SPMG

HEINEMANN MATHEMATICS 5

Answer book

These are the different types of pages in this book:

Heinemann

Heinemann Educational Publishers
Halley Court, Jordan Hill, Oxford OX2 8EJ
A division of Reed Educational and Professional Publishing Limited

MELBOURNE AUCKLAND FLORENCE
PRAGUE MADRID ATHENS SINGAPORE
TOKYO SÃO PAULO CHICAGO PORTSMOUTH (NH)
MEXICO IBADAN GABORONE JOHANNESBURG
KAMPALA NAIROBI

ISBN 0 435 03856 7

First published 1994
Revised 1995

97 98 99 10 9 8 7 6 5 4

Designed and produced by Bob Prescott Design Associates, Oxford

Printed in Great Britain by Thomson Litho Ltd, East Kilbride

1 Explorers

1 (a) 19 (b) 18 (c) 20
(d) 25 (e) 22 (f) 26 (g) 27
(h) 31 (i) 28 (j) 23 (k) 21

2 6,7,8,9

3 11 = 3 + 3 + 5
12 = 3 + 3 + 3 + 3
13 = 3 + 5 + 5
14 = 3 + 3 + 3 + 5
15 = 5 + 5 + 5
16 = 5 + 5 + 3 + 3
17 = 3 + 3 + 3 + 3 + 5
18 = 5 + 5 + 5 + 3
19 = 5 + 5 + 3 + 3 + 3
20 = 5 + 5 + 5 + 5

2 Explorers – *continued*

1 (a) 56 (b) 48 (c) 84 (d) 75
(e) 52 (f) 51 (g) 48 (h) 47
(i) 34 (j) 63 (k) 46 (l) 51

2 (a) 46 (b) 75 (c) 56 (d) 63
(e) 44 (f) 42 (g) 51 (h) 92
(i) 42 (j) 53 (k) 35 (l) 63
(m) 64 (n) 86 (o) 56 (p) 92

3 (a) 6 (b) 4 (c) 7
(d) 5 (e) 1 (f) 2

4 (a) 62 (b) 63 (c) 71 (d) 97
(e) 56 (f) 92 (g) 75 (h) 62
(i) 75 (j) 63 (k) 75 (l) 62

5 TURN BLUE DIAL ANTI-CLOCKWISE TO
TWO SIX EIGHT ONE NINE

3 The treasure trail

1 (a) 89 metres
(b) 102 metres
(c) 161 metres
(d) 149 metres

2 Answers will depend on children's choice of journeys.

3 (a) Kate 84 m – 55 m = 29 m
Tony 93 m – 28 m = 65 m
Lisa 77 m – 39 m = 38 m
Kelvin 70 m – 24 m = 46 m

4 (a) The owl started at Golden Pond.
(b) It passed the Silver Toadstool.

4 Crossing Ruby River

1 (a) 79 (b) 96 (c) 69 (d) 92
(e) 97 (f) 47 (g) 58 (h) 99
(i) 77 (j) 45 (k) 66 (l) 85

2 (a) 62 (b) 14 (c) 32 (d) 51
(e) 18 (f) 33 (g) 43 (h) 21
(i) 37 (j) 20 (k) 16 (l) 28

3 There are many correct additions and subtractions for each safe number.

4 The unsafe numbers are
38, 25, 90, 52, 93, 40, 55, 94, 19, 35.

5 The pyramid

1 (a) 590 (b) 425 (c) 405 (d) 644

2 (a) 192 (b) 194 (c) 309 (d) 288
(e) 172 (f) 383 (g) 168 (h) 176
(i) 477 (j) 276 (k) 114 (l) 239

3 E E O E E O

4 (a) 987
876
765
654
543
432

(b) Various examples could be chosen.
The two examples should have answers 321 and 210.

6 The treasure

1

(a)	(b)	(c)	(d)
210 + 438 648	648 − 196 452	452 + 475 927	927 − 179 748
(e)	**(f)**	**(g)**	**(h)**
210 − 97 113	113 + 384 497	497 + 156 653	653 − 140 513
(i)	**(j)**	**(k)**	**(l)**
210 − 186 24	24 + 399 423	423 − 195 228	228 + 247 475

2  (for answer 475)

The treasure – *continued* 6

3 (a) The sum of the digits in each answer is 9 (if the chosen digits were different).
(b) The sum of the digits in the answer is 18 (if the chosen digits were different).
The explorers will go to Emerald Forest ( represents 18).

Tree puzzles 7

1 (a) 600, 700, 800, 900, 1000, 1100
(b) 6400, 6300, 6200, 6100, 6000, 5900
(c) 500, 1000, 1500, 2000, 2500, 3000
(d) 2000, 1950, 1900, 1850, 1800, 1750

2 6697, 6796, 7696, 9676, 9766

3 (a) 5423
(b) 2354

4 (a) 3488
(b) 3550
(c) 3555
(d) 4444

8 Tree puzzles – *continued*

1 (a) 1462. (b) 4301. (c) 2067. (d) 6001.

2 Elm 6325 Ash 6415 Oak 7315

3 (a) Ash (b) Oak (c) Elm

4 (a) 500 (b) 4000 (c) 3

5 (a) 8 (b) 200 (c) 2000

6 (a) 2, 60, 700, 6000
(b) Answers depend on the children's choice of method.
(c) Various answers are possible, for example,
[1742.] + 8 → [1750.] + 50 → [1800.] + 200 → [2000.] + 6000 → [8000.]

9 Under the silver toadstool

1 (a) 1196 (b) 1584 (c) 1383
(d) 1439 (e) 1051 (f) 1337
(g) 1771 (h) 1524 (i) 1669

2 (a) 843 + 928 + 741 = 2512
(b) 455 + 596 + 843 = 1894
(c) 596 + 928 + 455 = 1979
(d) 741 + 843 + 455 = 2039

3 (a) Star, Rain and Sun were destroyed.
(b) Yes, 20 milllitrogs are still homeless.

10 The banquet

1 (a) 5988 (b) 8268 (c) 5175 (d) 8769

2 (a) 9191 (b) 6224 (c) 7306 (d) 8010

3 (a) 4203 (b) 5863
(c) 6804 (d) 7928
(e) 8650 (f) 9848

4 (a) ▲ → 3 ■ → 6 ● → 2
(b) 2623

11 The Great Store

1 (a) 3232
(b) 945
(c) 4864
(d) 1735
(e) 1845

2 (a) 1844
(b) 3609
(c) 2876
(d) 1587
(e) 3971

3 (a) 1718 (b) 4005 (c) 86 (d) 3215 (e) 3105

4 (a) 3672
(b) 534

12 Trog's Take-away

1 (a) 1995 (b) 3778 (c) 2678 (d) 877

2 (a) 1623 (b) 1433
(c) 2315 (d) 3790

3 (a) 2121 (b) 2563
(c) 438 (d) 1845

4 The following sacks have a difference of 1789:
8946 and 7157 (green and blue);
9013 and 7224 (lavender and yellow);
5367 and 3578 (brown and brown);
and 5471 and 3682 (red and purple).

13 Another adventure

1 Kate has £11·53 Tony has £19·05
Lisa has £17·11 Kelvin has £17·27

2 Various answers are possible, including:
(a) £10 + £1 + 20p + 5p
(b) £10 + £1 + £1 + 50p + 2p
(c) £10 + £5 + 50p + 20p + 10p + 2p + 2p
(d) £10 + £5 + £1 + 50p + 20p

3 (a) Kate £15·16 Tony £15·05 Lisa £14·04 Kelvin £15·09
(b) Kate £16·91 Tony £14·04 Lisa £16·07 Kelvin £16·05.

Another adventure – *continued* 14

1 (a) Various answers are possible. Change, using fewest notes and coins is as follows:

Lisa	5p, 20p, £1
Tony	2p, 10p, 20p, £1, £1
Kate	1p, 5p, 10p, 20p, £5
Kelvin	2p, 5p, 50p, £1, £1, £5

(b)

Lisa	£1·25 change
Tony	£2·32 change
Kate	£5·36 change
Kelvin	£7·57 change

2 (a) Various answers are possible. Change, using fewest notes and coins, is as follows:

Lisa	2p, 10p, £1, £1
Tony	1p, 10p, 50p, £5
Kate	1p, 2p, 5p, £1, £1, £5
Kelvin	5p, 10p, 50p, £1, £1, £1, £5

(b)

Lisa	£2·12
Tony	£5·61
Kate	£7·08
Kelvin	£8·65

3

Lisa	£9·13
Tony	£6·71
Kate	£8·28
Kelvin	£8·92

4 Lisa received £17 (3 x £5 + 4 x 50p).
Kate received £14 (2 x £5 + 8 x 50p).

15 Outward Bound

1 Kate £16·47
Kelvin £32·79
Lisa £28·01
Tony £26·40

2 £4·35

3 Answers depend on children's own choice of items.

4 £96·69

16 Outward Bound – *continued*

1 **(a)** £3·52 **(b)** £3·04 **(c)** £7·13

2 **(a)** £6·37 **(b)** £7·12
(c) £8·65 **(d)** £5·81

3 **(a)** correct **(b)** should be £22·61 **(c)** should be £21·17
(d) correct **(e)** should be £8·49 **(f)** should be £7·72
(g) correct **(h)** correct

4 Each person should pay £25 (100 ÷ 4).
Sammi is owed £4. Irfan owes £3.
Kate owes £7. Tony is owed £6.

There are several ways of sorting this out.
One way is as follows:
Kate gives £6 to Tony.
Kate gives £1 to Sammi.
Irfan gives £3 to Sammi.

Pairing 17

1 **(a)** 36
(b) 55

2 **(a)**

Consecutive numbers	How many numbers?	How many pairs?	Sum of each pair	Total
1 to 6	6	3	7	21
1 to 8	8	4	9	36
1 to 10	10	5	11	55

(b) One possible rule is:
Multiply the number of pairs by the sum of each pair.

3 **(a)** 78 (6 x 13) **(b)** 210 (10 x 21) **(c)** 5050 (50 x 101)
(d) 81 (3 x 27) **(e)** 255 (5 x 51)

4 **(a)** 45 [(4 x 9) + 9] **(b)** 91 [(6 x 13) + 13]
(c) 98 [(3 x 27) + 17] **(d)** 315 [(4 x 69) + 39]

Magazines 18

1 **(a)** 12 **(b)** 20 **(c)** 24 **(d)** 32
(e) 28 **(f)** 35 **(g)** 42 **(h)** 56
(i) 40 **(j)** 60 **(k)** 70 **(l)** 90
(m) 18 **(n)** 27 **(o)** 63 **(p)** 90
(q) 12 **(r)** 42 **(s)** 54 **(t)** 60

2 **(a)** Sara **(b)** 1 more

3 **(a)** 36 pages → 9 copies of Emma's magazine
or 6 copies of Steve's magazine
(b) 49 pages → 7 copies of Ben's magazine
38 pages → 2 copies of Sara's magazine
and 2 copies of Shamina's magazine
Other answers are possible for 38 pages.

19 Class copies

1 (a) 81 (b) 135 (c) 216 (d) 189
(e) 62 (f) 124 (g) 217 (h) 186
(i) 144 (j) 216 (k) 240 (l) 192
(m) 90 (n) 180 (o) 240 (p) 270
(q) 203 (r) 261 (s) 116 (t) 290

2 The answer depends on the size of the class.

3 4 pages

4 (a) Ms Smith's class
(b) 5 pages

20 Record Breakers

1 Jenny 990 metres
Shamina 440 metres
Sharon 770 metres
Sara 550 metres
Ben 660 metres

2 Sue 434 metres
Emma 651 metres
Steve 868 metres
Ben 1085 metres

3 Kay 296 metres
David 742 metres
Jonathan 824 metres
Paulo 690 metres
Maria 496 metres
Yasmeen 791 metres

Collectors 21

1 Emma 960 stickers
Fiona 928 model cars
Lewis 910 postcards
Peter 960 books

2 (a) 750 stamps
(b) 890 stamps
(c) 994 stamps
(d) 992 stamps

3 (a) 1260 coins
(b) 1000 coins

4 (a) Jenny has 1308 photos
(b) John has 1380 photos
(c) William has 1323 photos
(d) Caroline has 1314 photos
John should win the prize.

5 120 tapes (15 full racks of 8)

Spotlight on Sharon 22

1 (a) 3285 days
(b) 2555 days
(c) 2190 days

2 (a) 1095 step-ups
(b) 1825 stretches
(c) 2920 sit-ups
(d) 1460 handstands
(e) 3650 press-ups

3 (a) 600 minutes
(b) 1500 minutes
(c) 420 minutes
(d) 4200 minutes
(e) 840 minutes

22 Spotlight on Sharon – *continued*

4 **(a)** 260 hours **(b)** 1560 hours

5 Hazel is 18 years old.

23 Bundles

1 **(a)** 150 sheets **(b)** 210 sheets **(c)** 370 sheets

2 **(a)** 260 sheets **(b)** 390 sheets **(c)** 300 sheets **(d)** 280 sheets

3 100 sheets

4 **(a)** 900 sheets **(b)** 2300 sheets **(c)** 3000 sheets **(d)** 3500 sheets

5 A possible rule is:
To multiply by 100, move each digit two places to the left and put zeros in the tens and units places.

6 **(a)** 4600 **(b)** 8100 **(c)** 9700 **(d)** 6000
(e) 5700 **(f)** 9200 **(g)** 8500 **(h)** 440
(i) 660 **(j)** 5900 **(k)** 530 **(l)** 7100

24 Speedprint

1 3966 copies

2 *Scream* 2644 copies
Puzzles 6372 copies
Champs 8832 copies
Monster 4984 copies
Soaps 5295 copies

3 **(a)** 6828 sheets **(b)** 6870 sheets **(c)** 6936 sheets

Speedprint – *continued* 24

4 *Cool* 6444 sheets
Galaxy 7742 sheets
Charts 8106 sheets
Donna 9336 sheets
Stars 9738 sheets

5 *Donna* 9552 sheets
Stars 9531 sheets
Donna uses 21 more sheets.

At the printer's 25

1 £3372

2 *Scream* £2248
Puzzles £6860
Champs £9925
Monster £9728
Soaps £9415

3 4635
x 2
9270p → £92·70

4 **(a)** £98·25
(b) £99·20
(c) £96·80
(d) £99·54
(e) £99·45
(f) £99·76

5 Largs £80·70
Girvan £62·76
Falkirk £99·96
Renton £99·12
Paisley £97·92

26 Making copies

1 (a) 540 sheets (b) 1020 sheets (c) 1245 sheets (d) 1485 sheets

2 (a)

Mini	Midi	Maxi	Super
900	1700	2075	2475

(b)

Mini	Midi	Maxi	Super
1548	2924	3569	4257

(c)

Mini	Midi	Maxi	Super
2160	4080	4980	5940

3 100 minutes or 1 hour 40 minutes

4 (a) 5395 copies
(b) No, it would take 65 minutes.

5 The Super

6 5307 + 648 = 5955

7 Answer depends on the school copier.

27 Magazine costs

1

	Mr Kidd	Mrs Watt	Ms Smith	Mr Reed	Mrs Anwar
(a)	£28·35	£32·55	£25·20	£31·50	£30·45
(b)	£30·51	£35·03	£27·12	£33·90	£32·77
(c)	£36·99	£42·47	£32·88	£41·10	£39·73

2 (a) £94·53 (b) £131·52 (c) £197·28

3 (a) £214·50
(b) £346·50
(c) £136·50 + £126 = £262·50

Magazine costs – *continued* 27

4 (a) £565
(b) £286·50
(c) £425
(d)

Advertising	£286·50
Sales	+ £425·00
School takes in	£711·50
Printing	– £565·00
Profit	£146·50

The magazine makes a profit.

Orders 28

1

	(a) 140	(b) 251	(c) 237
(d) 179	(e) 239	(f) 189	(g) 207
(h) 252	(i) 123	(j) 315	(k) 502

2

	(a) 141	(b) 231	(c) 356
(d) 475	(e) 167	(f) 281	(g) 408
(h) 160	(i) 316	(j) 394	(k) 503

3

	(a) 140	(b) 180	(c) 270
(d) 190	(e) 260	(f) 290	(g) 150
(h) 120	(i) 180	(j) 210	(k) 230

29 Magazine sales

1 Autumn 200 copies
Winter 300 copies
Spring 300 copies
Summer 400 copies

2 (a) 400 (b) 800 (c) 600 (d) 600 (e) 400 (f) 100

3 Autumn 220 copies
Winter 280 copies
Spring 340 copies
Summer 390 copies

4 (a) 420 (b) 640 (c) 780 (d) 550 (e) 390 (f) 150

5 They are both correct. 225 is mid-way between 220 and 230.

6 (a) 260 or 270 (b) 310 or 320 (c) 40 or 50
(d) 80 or 90 (e) 510 (f) 690
(g) 900 or 910 (h) 740 or 750 (i) 650 or 660
(j) 420 (k) 300 (l) 900

30 Magazine sales – *continued*

1 (a) about 150 (b) about 190 (c) about 160
(d) about 180 (e) about 280 or 290 (f) about 150
(g) about 360 or 370 (h) about 240 (i) about 130
(j) about 470 or 480 (k) about 290 (l) about 200

2 (a) about 130 (b) about 110 (c) about 170
(d) about 150 (e) about 220 or 230 (f) about 300 or 310
(g) about 260 (h) about 320 (i) about 260
(j) about 310 (k) about 420 (l) about 100

3 (a) about 190 magazines
(b) about 130 more magazines

Sales 31

1 *Puzzles, Champs, Cool, Upbeat*

2 *Scream, Puzzles, Champs, Upbeat, Donna*

3 (a)

Scream	3345 copies	*Cool*	4608 copies
Puzzles	4584 copies	*Upbeat*	3831 copies
Champs	4570 copies	*Donna*	3098 copies
Monster	4204 copies	*Stars*	6000 copies
Soaps	5555 copies	*Galaxy*	4281 copies

(b) *Stars*

(c) 2655 more than *Scream*
1416 more than *Puzzles*
1430 more than *Champs*
1796 more than *Monster*
445 more than *Soaps*
1392 more than *Cool*
2169 more than *Upbeat*
2902 more than *Donna*
1719 more than *Galaxy*

(d) These magazines increased their sales:
Monsters by 1036 copies
Soaps by 183 copies
Stars by 942 copies
Galaxy by 1643 copies
Galaxy had the greatest increase.

4 (a)

Scream	2155 more copies	*Cool*	892 more copies
Puzzles	916 more copies	*Upbeat*	1669 more copies
Champs	930 more copies	*Donna*	2402 more copies
Monster	1296 more copies	*Stars*	no more copies
Soaps	no more copies	*Galaxy*	1219 more copies

(b) *Donna* (2353 copies in January, 745 in February and 2402 in March)

32 Naomi's numbers

1 The answer, 495, contains the same three digits as the other numbers.

$$\begin{array}{r} 954 \\ -\ 459 \\ \hline 495 \end{array}$$

(This subtraction 'repeats' if the process is continued.)

2 Each answer becomes 495 (and then 'repeats').

3 (a) The answer becomes 6174 (and then 'repeats').
(b) These 4-digit numbers also give an answer of 6174 (and then 'repeat').

33 The number wheel

Answers depend on numbers thrown during the game.

34 Woodgreen Carnival

1 (a) 7 planks (b) 7 helpers
(c) 9 flags (d) 8 balloons

2 (a) 9 stars in each row and 1 left over
(b) 8 nails in each row and 1 left over
(c) 10 chairs in each row and 2 left over
(d) 9 lights in each row and 4 left over

3 (a) 4 r 1 (b) 6 r 1 (c) 6 (d) 8 r 1
(e) 10 (f) 1 r 3 (g) 9 r 2 (h) 6 r 3
(i) 5 r 1 (j) 5 r 2 (k) 8 (l) 4 r 2
(m) 5 (n) 4 (o) 9 (p) 5

4 30 or 60 or 90…

35 Getting ready

1 (a) 43 flowers (b) 27 balloons (c) 19 rosettes

2 (a) 23 police (b) 14 traffic wardens (c) 26 stewards

3 (a) 17 tickets (b) 14 programmes (c) 17 badges (and 2 left over)

4 (a) 14 sets (b) 13 sets (c) 18 sets and 1 left over

5 (a) 21 r 2 (b) 17 r 1 (c) 37 r 1 (d) 15 r 4
(e) 46 r 1 (f) 23 r 1 (g) 13 r 3 (h) 16 r 3
(i) 29 (j) 15 (k) 27 (l) 19

6 (a) 18 minutes (b) 28 minutes

7 (a) 18 tapes (b) 12 tapes (c) 9 tapes

36 Getting ready – *continued*

1 (a) 36 (b) 107 (c) 80 (d) 71 (e) 61 (and 4 left over)

2 (a) 109 (b) 43 (and 3 left over) (c) 68 (d) 140
(e) 76 (and 1 left over)

3 (a) 38 (b) 69 (c) 57 (and 2 left over) (d) 157
(e) 53 (and 1 left over)

4 (a) 125 (b) 85 (c) 153 (and 1 left over)
(d) 176 (and 1 left over) (e) 292

5 (a) 309 (b) 206 (c) 393 r 1 (d) 196 r 3
(e) 177 r 1 (f) 471 r 1 (g) 129 r 4 (h) 170 r 2

6 (a) 777 , 402 , 417
(b) 777 , 521 , 417

7 (a) Some of the following: 125, 165, 215, 265, 615, 625
(b) Some of the following: 152, 162, 512, 562, 612, 652
(c) Some of the following: 251, 521

37 Dragons galore!

1 **(a)** 4 m **(b)** 6 m **(c)** 7 m
(d) 9 m **(e)** 8 m **(f)** 10 m

2 **(a)** 3 hoops **(b)** 5 feathers **(c)** 6 balls of wool
(d) 2 tubes **(e)** 9 cards **(f)** 10 sheets of foil

3 **(a)** 3 **(b)** 4 r 2 **(c)** 1 r 4 **(d)** 8 r 4
(e) 4 r 1 **(f)** 6 r 3 **(g)** 1 r 6 **(h)** 7
(i) 5 r 3 **(j)** 5 **(k)** 2 r 5 **(l)** 10 r 1

4 **(a)** 5 bags (and 3 nuts left over)
(b) 8 bundles (and 2 straws left over)
(c) 7 strings (and 5 bottle tops left over)

5 There are 6 plates for each dragon. There are 2 left.

6 One dragon has 14 teeth, the rest have 9 each.

38 Dragons galore! – *continued*

1 **(a)** 14 bows **(b)** 16 corks **(c)** 13 cotton reels
(d) 114 beads **(e)** 139 buttons **(f)** 94 bells (and 1 left over)

2 **(a)** 12 tartan **(b)** 14 striped **(c)** 11 red (and 4 left over)
(d) 108 spotted **(e)** 64 checked **(f)** 71 pink (and 3 left over)

3 **(a)** 15 **(b)** 123 r 6 **(c)** 154 r 1 **(d)** 14 r 1
(e) 147 r 2 **(f)** 113 r 4 **(g)** 142 r 5 **(h)** 105
(i) 33 r 2 **(j)** 46 **(k)** 117 r 3 **(l)** 130 r 5

4 **(a)** 70 patches (5 petals left) **(b)** 101 patches (2 stars left)
(c) 107 patches (1 circle left)

5 76 peach, 16 white, 24 lilac flowers

6 50 pink flowers

Street Decorations 39

1 **(a)** 8 carnations **(b)** 5 tulips **(c)** 2 roses
(d) 3 daffodils **(e)** 10 daisies **(f)** 6 pansies

2 **(a)** 4 **(b)** 7 **(c)** 5 **(d)** 9 **(e)** 10 **(f)** 6

3 **(a)** 4 **(b)** 2 r 6 **(c)** 6 r 2 **(d)** 8 r 4
(e) 4 r 2 **(f)** 1 r 7 **(g)** 7 r 3 **(h)** 1
(i) 6 r 5 **(j)** 9 **(k)** 10 r 3 **(l)** 9 r 1

4 **(a)** 3 rows (and 8 bottles left over)
(b) 8 groups (and 4 bells left over)
(c) 9 sets (and 7 pipes left over)

5 **(a)** 6 lamp-posts **(b)** 5 jesters
Some children may consider **two** sides of Glebe Street and give answers of
(a) 12 lamp-posts **(b)** 10 jesters

40 Street decorations – *continued*

1 (a) 11 bows (b) 12 ribbons (and 3 left over)
(c) 24 sheets of card (d) 108 lights (and 7 left over)
(e) 37 boxes (and 4 left over) (f) 121 bits of tinsel (and 2 left over)

2 (a) 11 red (b) 17 yellow (c) 106 orange
(d) 78 green (and 1 left over) (e) 36 blue (and 8 left over)
(f) 110 white (and 7 left over)

3 (a) 11 r 2 (b) 11 r 1 (c) 109 r 7 (d) 62 r 4
(e) 86 r 3 (f) 46 r 6 (g) 118 r 5 (h) 12
(i) 121 (j) 99 r 4 (k) 100 r 7 (l) 109 r 8

4 (a) 19 triangles
(b) 17 circles
(c) 25 rectangles

5 (a) Paula has 70 candles.
(b) She has 8 sets, with 6 candles left.

6 (a) The jester is correct.
The sum of the digits of 576 is 5 + 7 + 6 = 18.
18 divides exactly by 9.

(b)

Number	Divides exactly by 9?	Sum of digits	Divides exactly by 9?
279	yes	18	yes
630	yes	9	yes
747	yes	18	yes
819	yes	18	yes

(c) 648, 702

Litter 41

1 (a) 6 cups (b) 8 cans (c) 10 leaflets
(d) 9 bottles (and 4 left over) (e) 7 packets (and 5 left over)
(f) 6 cartons (and 6 left over) (g) 9 tubs
(h) 8 newspapers (and 3 left over) (i) 5 wrappers (and 2 left over)

2 (a) 23 cans and (d) 103 cans

3 (a) 17 (b) 28 (c) 31 (and 5 magazines left over)
(d) 49 (and 4 newspapers left over)
(e) 67 (and 5 posters left over) (f) 80

4 Move the digits one place to the right.
The units digit becomes the remainder.

5 (a) 8 r 7 (b) 12 r 6 (c) 30 r 9 (d) 97 r 9

6 (b) 450 (e) 900

7 Any ticket with a number whose unit digit is 7.
For example: 7, 17, 27, 37…

The procession 42

1 (a) 142 (and 5 spectators left over) (b) 113 (and 2 marchers left over)
(c) 40 (and 6 jugglers left over) (d) 71 (and 5 musicians left over)
(e) 12 (and 6 jesters left over) (f) 37 (and 6 acrobats left over)

2 (a) 122 (b) 113 (c) 15 (d) 75 (e) 31

3 (a) 6 (b) 0 (c) 1 (d) 7 (e) 2

4 (a) 3 (b) 1 (c) 1 (d) 1 (e) 1

5 (a) 70 bottles (b) 9 bottles (c) 16 bottles

6 There are 27 drummers.

43 Carnival

1 C → 120
a → 71
r → 50
n → 55
i → 55
v → 92
a → 67
l → 103

2 325 tickets were sold.

3

Red Flash	£2·06 each
Blue Streak	£1·86 each
Silver Cloud	£2·26 each
Golden Shower	£2·27 each
Orange Burst	£1·50 each

4 **(a)** The box of 8 is the best value, because each firework costs £2·12.
In the box of 6, each firework costs £2·15, and in the box of 10, each firework costs £2·20.
(b) The cheapest way is to buy 3 boxes of 6, which cost £38·70.

Carnival jewellery 44

1 **(a)** 5 parts – $\frac{2}{5}$ **(b)** 4 parts – $\frac{2}{4}$
(c) 9 parts – $\frac{3}{9}$ **(d)** 7 parts – $\frac{4}{7}$
(e) 6 parts – $\frac{2}{6}$ **(f)** 8 parts – $\frac{4}{8}$

2 **(a)** $\frac{6}{8}$, $\frac{2}{8}$ **(b)** $\frac{2}{6}$, $\frac{4}{6}$
(c) $\frac{5}{9}$, $\frac{4}{9}$ **(d)** $\frac{2}{7}$, $\frac{5}{7}$

3 **(a)** $\frac{7}{9}$ **(b)** $\frac{5}{7}$
(c) $\frac{4}{6}$ **(d)** $\frac{5}{8}$

4 Answers depend on the children's designs.
$\frac{4}{9}$ of design should be blue.

More carnival jewels 45

1 **(a)** $\frac{5}{6}$ and $\frac{5}{8}$
(b) $\frac{1}{6}$

2 **(a)** $\frac{4}{7}$ and $\frac{5}{9}$
(b) $\frac{1}{9}$

3

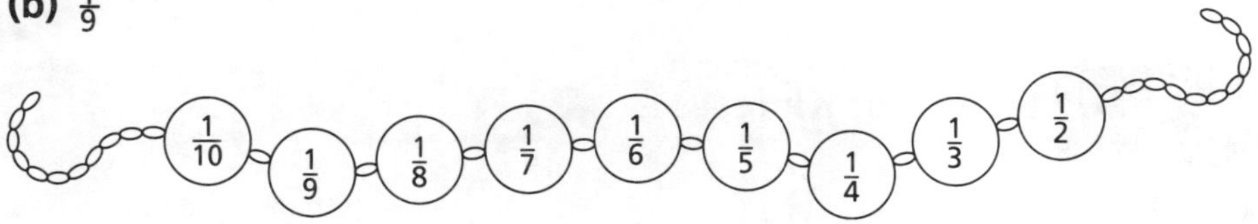

4 Answer depends on the children's choice of design.
The hairclips should be divided into sixths.

5 **(a)** 5 **(b)** 7 **(c)** 9
(d) 5 **(e)** 9 **(f)** 5
(g) 4 **(h)** 9 **(i)** 8

6 **(a)** 8 are gold **(b)** 6 are silver **(c)** 34 are copper

46 Patterns and puzzles

1 **(a), (b), (c)**

x	1	2	3	4	5
1	1	2	3	4	5
2	2	4	0	2	4
3	3	0	3	0	3
4	4	2	0	4	2
5	5	4	3	2	1

(d) Possible answers include:
1st row same as 1st column.
2nd row same as 2nd column,
and so on…

1st row is same as 5th row reversed.
2nd row is same as 4th row reversed, and so on…

3rd row and 3rd column are symmetrical.
The table is symmetrical about each diagonal.

2 Red

3 **(a)** +
(b) x
(c) ÷
(d) x
(e) –
(f) ÷
(g) ÷ and ÷

4 **(a)** 7
(b) 8
(c) 8
(d) 9
(e) 9

47 Professor Kluless

1 **(a)** 3 x 37 = 111
6 x 37 = 222
9 x 37 = 333
12 x 37 = 444

(b) The three digits of each answer are the same.
The digits increase by 1 from one answer to the next.

Professor Kluless – *continued* 47

(c) 15 x 37 = 555
18 x 37 = 666
21 x 37 = 777
24 x 37 = 888
27 x 37 = 999 Collect **I**

2 **(a)** 53 + 36 + 29 = 118
(b) 53 + 36 – 29 = 60
(c) 53 x 36 – 29 = 1879
(d) 53 x 36 + 29 = 1937
+ is used most often. Collect **C**

3 He planted 1206 altogether. Collect **U**

Zantha 48

4 Zantha's number is 621 Collect **R**

5 1st offer = £128 2nd offer = £136
The 2nd offer is better. Collect **VERY**

6 He ordered 4 plain and 8 spotted ties.
Collect **YYYs**

7 The message is **I C U R VERY YYYs**
(*"I see you are very wise."*)

49 The Professor's safe

1

Colour		Answer	Colour		Answer
Red	→	245	Orange	→	601
Purple	→	49	Orange	→	952
Green	→	490	Green	→	238
Blue	→	70	Green	→	4760
Yellow	→	1000	Yellow	→	595
Yellow	→	302	Blue	→	1001

2 Possible answers include:

(a)

5 – 5 = 0	5 + 5 = 10
5 – 4 = 1	55 – 44 = 11
4 + 4 + 4 – 5 – 5 = 2	4 + 4 + 4 = 12
4 + 4 – 5 = 3	5 + 4 + 4 = 13
4	5 + 5 + 4 = 14
5	5 + 5 + 5 = 15
5 + 5 – 4 = 6	4 x 4 = 16
4 + 4 + 4 – 5 = 7	4 + 4 + 4 + 5 = 17
4 + 4 = 8	5 + 5 + 4 + 4 = 18
5 + 4 = 9	5 + 5 + 5 + 4 = 19
	5 x 4 = 20

(b) 5 x 5 x 4 = 100 *or* 55 + 44 + 5 – 4 = 100

3 (a) 217 → 103 → 99 → 124 Total 543

(b) 126 → 133 → 49 → 88 Total 396

(c) Any one of these paths:

217 → 133 → 84 → 161	126 → 133 → 84 → 161
231 → 77 → 49 → 161	217 → 133 → 49 → 161
126 → 133 → 49 → 161	217 → 77 → 49 → 161
126 → 77 → 49 → 161	

50 The Kluless Game

Answers depend on choices during the games.

HANNAH and BOB 51

1 There are many possible answers.

2 (a) 13 + 31 = 44, one step

(b) 56 + 65 = 121, one step

(c) 48 + 84 = 132; 132 + 231 = 363, two steps

(d) 95 + 59 = 154; 154 + 451 = 605; 605 + 506 = 1111, three steps

3 Answers depend on the children's choice of numbers.

4 128 and 1356 are one-step numbers,
658 is a two-step number,
263 is a three-step number.

5 (a), (b), (c) Various answers are possible.

Lewis Water 52

1 6 tenths, 0·6

2

	Sea Mist	Swift	Spray	Swan
(a)	0·7	0·9	0·2	0·5
(b)	0·3	0·1	0·8	0·5

3 (a) 2·8 pizzas (b) 3·1 packs of yoghurt tubs

4 (a) 0·9 (b) 0·5 (c) 0·3 (d) 3·1
(e) 2·7 (f) 7·2 (g) 4·5

53 Balloon trip over Lewis Water

1 (a) 14 tenths (b) 19 tenths (c) 28 tenths
(d) 35 tenths (e) 50 tenths

2 (a) 2 units and 9 tenths = 2·9
(b) 1 unit and 8 tenths = 1·8
(c) 4 units and 7 tenths = 4·7
(d) 3 units and 0 tenths = 3·0

3 4·0, 3·2, 2·1, 2·0, 1·2, 0·7, 0·4

4 (a) 5 tenths (b) 2 tens (c) 0 tenths (d) 8 units

54 Boat repairs

1 (a) 4·1m (b) 8·3m (c) 3·2m (d) 5·3m (e) 4·0m

2 (a) 7·1m (b) 8·2m
(c) 8·6m (d) 7·2m
(e) 8·9m (f) 8·0m

3 The rope was 26·3m long.

4 (a) 39·1m (b) 47·0m (c) 66·9m
(d) 43·0m (e) 71·3m

5 The red rope was 38·2m long.
The blue rope was 66·5m long.

6 (a) 5·3m + 3·2m + 4·4m (= 12·9m)
(b) 7·6m + 5·3m + 2·9m (= 15·8m)

Model boat races 55

1 *Fairwind* is
(a) 0·3m longer than *Hope*
(b) 0·1m longer than *Storm*
(c) 0·4m longer than *Dawn*
(d) 0·5m longer than *Imp*

2 (a) *Imp* is the shortest.
(b) *Imp* is
0·3m shorter than *Sprite*
0·5m shorter than *Fairwind*
0·2m shorter than *Hope*
0·4m shorter than *Storm*
0·1m shorter than *Dawn*

3 *Imp* is 1·5m shorter
Fairwind is 1·0m shorter
Hope is 1·3m shorter
Storm is 1·1m shorter
Dawn is 1·4m shorter

4 *Sprite* has sailed 8·8m
Fairwind has sailed 9·0m
Hope has sailed 8·3m
Imp has sailed 8·5m

5 (a) 7·6 (b) 5·6 (c) 5·8 (d) 0·8 (e) 3·1

56 Model boat races – *continued*

1 *Sprite* is 11·6m from the finish
Dawn is 1·5m from the finish
Imp is 7·2m from the finish
Storm is 5·1m from the finish
Hope is 5·7m from the finish
Fairwind is 13·6m from the finish

2 A to B is 14·6m
B to C is 10·8m
C to D is 13·6m
D to E is 16·3m
E to F is 15·3m
F to G is 11·9m

3 **(a)** 11·8 **(b)** 10·3 **(c)** 11·5 **(d)** 8·9 **(e)** 54·7

4 **(a)** 13·6 **(b)** 18·3 **(c)** 22·3
(d) 42·9 **(e)** 89·4 **(f)** 64·6

5 **(a)** 0·5 **(b)** 2·3 **(c)** 13·5 **(d)** 7·0

6 red boat 0·9m
blue boat 0·7m
green boat 0·5m

57 Captain Hawkins' souvenir shop

1 **(a)** The shelf is 2·4m long.
(b) The shelf is 2·5m long.

2 **(a)** 1·8m **(b)** 4·2m **(c)** 5·6m **(d)** 8·1m
(e) 1·4m **(f)** 1·6m **(g)** 1·8m **(h)** 7·2m
(i) 5·4m **(j)** 4·0m

3 **(a)** 6·9m **(b)** 4·8m **(c)** 6·8m **(d)** 9·6m

Paddle power 58

1 Jason's canoe travels 19·2m
Eric's canoe travels 30·6m
Monica's canoe travels 15·6m
Carmen's canoe travels 13·3m

2 **(a)** 54·4m **(b)** 33·5m **(c)** 30·0m **(d)** 13·5m
(e) 46·9m **(f)** 24·5m **(g)** 22·5m **(h)** 15·6m
(i) 25·8m **(j)** 50·4m **(k)** 22·8m **(l)** 17·8m

3 **(a)** 52·8 **(b)** 84·6 **(c)** 85·6 **(d)** 82·8
(e) 94·5 **(f)** 97·0 **(g)** 99·4 **(h)** 98·4

4 **(a)** Jason 10 x 2·4m = 24m Eric 10 x 2·6m = 26m
Monica 10 x 3·4m = 34m Carmen 10 x 1·9m = 19m
(b) When you multiply by 10, the digits move one place to the left. This may be expressed in other ways.

5 **(a)** 57 **(b)** 89
(c) 6 **(d)** 8
(e) 155 **(f)** 307

Spick and span 59

1 **(a)** Each strip is 0·4m long.
(b) Each strip is 0·3m long.

2 **(a)** 2·4 litres **(b)** 2·3 litres
(c) 1·6 litres **(d)** 1·7 litres

3 **(a)** 2·8 **(b)** 2·6 **(c)** 3·3 **(d)** 0·9
(e) 1·2 **(f)** 1·6 **(g)** 6·2 **(h)** 4·7

4 **(a)** 2·9m **(b)** 2·9m **(c)** 4·2m **(d)** 3·7m
(e) 5·7m **(f)** 0·9m **(g)** 3·9m **(h)** 1·8m

60 Decked out

1 (a) 3·5m (b) 3·6m (c) 8·5m (d) 12·5m (e) 16·5m (f) 13·8m

2 (a) 10·5 (b) 14·6 (c) 28·3 (d) 14·2
(e) 8·4 (f) 49·5 (g) 11·3 (h) 9·9

3 (a) 2·3, 4·5, 7·1, 19·4
(b) To divide by 10, move the digits one place to the right.
This may be expressed in other ways.
(c) 3·4, 6·6, 8·0, 40·4

4 (a) Yes, it is magic.

(b)

2·4	0·3	1·8
0·9	1·5	2·1
1·2	2·7	0·6

(c) Yes. Each row, column and diagonal has the same total (4·5).

61 Taking stock

1 (a)

Number of boxes	1	2	3	4	5	6	7	8	9	10
Number of caps	15	30	45	60	75	90	105	120	135	150

(b) 6 boxes 90
7 boxes +105
13 boxes 195 caps

(c) Any two of these ways:

5 boxes 75
8 boxes +120
13 boxes 195 caps

4 boxes 60
9 boxes +135
13 boxes 195 caps

3 boxes 45
10 boxes +150
13 boxes 195 caps

Taking stock – *continued* 61

2

Number of boxes	1	2	3	4	5	6	7	8	9	10
Number of stickers	18	36	54	72	90	108	126	144	162	180

4 boxes 72
10 boxes +180
14 boxes 252 stickers

3 (a) 272 floats (b) 504 hooks
(c) 576 flies (d) 234 lines
(e) 240 floats (f) 798 hooks
(g) 396 flies (h) 324 lines

Lewis Water Canoe Club 62

1 (a) £280 (b) £820 (c) £520
(d) £960 (e) £510 (f) £420
(g) £780 (h) £840 (i) £700

2 (a) £420 (b) £700 (c) £1040
(d) £680 (e) £700 (f) £5580
(g) £2870 (h) £2560 (i) £2340

3 (a) The item is a paddle.
(b) The answer depends on the method used.
For example, 29 is about 30
30 x 20 = 600, so the item costs about £20.
Try the paddle: 29 x £21 = £609, which is correct.

63 Regatta on Lewis Water

1 (a)

Number of circuits	1	2	3	4	5	10	20	30
Course distance	32 m	64 m	96 m	128 m	160 m	320 m	640 m	960 m

(b)

```
 32m        32m
x 4        x 30
128m       960m
```

(c)
21 circuits ——— 672m
25 circuits ——— 800m
32 circuits ——— 1024m
35 circuits ——— 1120m

2 (a)

```
 35m       35m       140m
x 4       x 20       700m
140m      700m       840m
```

(b)

```
 28m       28m        56m
x 2       x 30     + 840m
 56m      840m       896m
```

(c)

```
 46m       46m        46m
x 1       x 20     + 920m
 46m      920m       966m
```

(d)

```
 25m       25m        25m
x 1       x 30     + 750m
 25m      750m       775m
```

(e)

```
 37m       37m       111m
x 3       x 20     + 740m
111m      740m       851m
```

(f)

```
 43m       43m        86m
x 2       x 20     + 860m
 86m      860m       946m
```

3 **20** and **36** **30** and **24** **45** and **16**

Lady of Lewis 64

1 **(a)** 253 passengers **(b)** 391 passengers
(c) 299 passengers **(d)** 437 passengers

2 **(a)** £527 **(b)** 624 weeks **(c)** 384 hours **(d)** 396 cartons
(e) 396 bags **(f)** £646 **(g)** £375

Pirate treasure 65

72	42	405	405	168	432

570	72	168	480	8600

42	480

432	672	2106	8600	72

672	4700

4700	672	2106	8600

The message is:
HIDDEN CHEST IS NORTH OF FORT
The treasure is in Captain's cave.

Decimoles 66

1
(a) 10·5
(b) 63
(c) 9
(d) 5·8

2
(a) 36·8
(b) subtract 7·9
(c) add 6·6
(d) subtract 28·4 or divide by 5

3
(a) subtract 6·4 or divide by 3
(b) add 4·9
(c) multiply by 10 or add 72·9
(d) divide by 2 or subtract 40·5

67 Pooling ideas

1 Answers could include long tape, metre stick, trundle wheel etc.

2 (a), (b), (c) Answers depend on the size of the school hall.

3 (a), (b), (c), (d) Answers depend on the size of the school's netball court and dining room.

4 **(a)** Answer depends on the size of the school playground.
(b) Answers will vary.

68 Pooling ideas – *continued*

1 25m or 50m. Each race distance will be a whole number of lengths.

2 **(a)** 10 lengths
(b) 50m freestyle. This race would be $2\frac{1}{2}$ lengths of St Andrew's pool. It would finish in the middle of the pool.

3 **(a)** Lara swam 33m
Rob swam 66m
Karen swam 132m
(b) Practical work
(c) Practical work

4 64 metres

5 96 metres

St Andrew's School pool 69

1 **(a)** The depth at the shallow end is 70cm.
The depth at the deep end is 130cm.
(b), **(c)** The answers depend on the child's measurements.

2 (a), (b), (c), (d) The answers depend on the child's measurements.

3 (a), (b), (c) The answers depend on the teacher's and child's measurements.

4 Practical drawing work.
Possible rectangles:

11 cm x 1 cm	10 cm x 2 cm
9 cm x 3 cm	8 cm x 4 cm
7 cm x 5 cm	6 cm x 6 cm

Glides and dives 70

1 Naomi – 4 metres and 35 centimetres
Kris – 4 metres and 97 centimetres
Gordon – 376 centimetres
Marie – 429 centimetres
Rashmi – 304 centimetres

2 **(a)** Naomi – 7 m 81 cm
Kris – 9 m 9 cm
Gordon – 6 m 81 cm
Marie – 7 m 28 cm
Rashmi – 7 m 4 cm
(b) The winner is Kris.
Next are Naomi and Marie.

70 Glides and dives – *continued*

3 (a) The difference in depth is:

Naomi	84 cm
Kris	1 m 16 cm or 116 cm
Gordon	1 m 25 cm or 125 cm
Marie	34 cm
Jan	1 m 11 cm or 111 cm

(b) The deepest dive is Gordon's – 2 m 14 cm

The difference in depth is:

Naomi	41 cm
Kris	9 cm
Marie	91 cm
Jan	14 cm
Rashmi	1 m 25 cm or 125 cm

71 In at the deep end

1 (a) 10

(b) $\frac{1}{10}$

2 The answers depend on the objects measured.

3 The answers depend on the answers to Q2.

4 (a) 2 tiles – 0·6 m 3 tiles – 0·8 m

(b) 7 tiles

Junior Rangers 72

1 (a) $13\frac{1}{2}$ cm^2 (b) 8 cm^2 (c) 11 cm^2

2 (a) Answers depend on badges drawn by the children.

(b) Practical drawing work. The square badge should have side length 6 cm.

(c) Practical drawing work. The rectangular badge is likely to have these sizes: $7\frac{1}{2}$ cm x 3 cm or 5 cm x $4\frac{1}{2}$ cm

3 (a) 16 cm^2

(b), (c), (d) Practical work on **centimetre** squared grids.

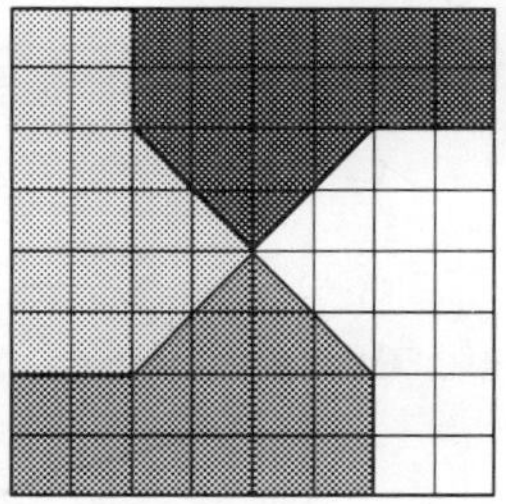

(e) 64 cm^2

Carol's Carpets 73

1 Practical work

2 (a) Answer depends on the size of the desk.

(b) Practical work

3 (a) Practical work

(b) 1 metre or 100 centimetres

4 (a), (b), (c) } Answers depend on the children and the objects used.

5 (a), (b), (c) } Various answers are possible.

74 Carol's Carpets – *continued*

6 **(a)** 1 square metre
(b) Two of these possible shapes:

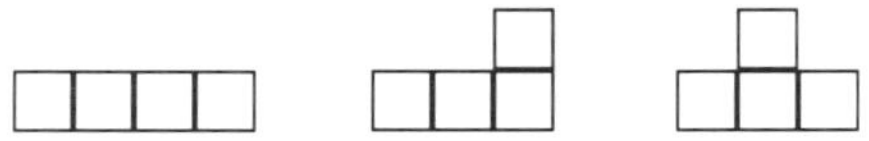

7 Practical work

8 **(a)** She needs 12 m^2 of carpet.
(b) No. The wall is 8 m^2 and she has only enough paint to cover $6m^2$.

75 The Kluless laboratory

1 **(a)**, **(b)**, **(c)** } Answers depend on the children's choice of object.

2 **(a)** sludge (350g) **(b)** nettles (170g)
(c) yuck (80g) **(d)** thorns (125g)
(e) slime (265g) **(f)** squidge (205g)

3 **(a)** 500g, 20g, 10g
(b) 20g, 10g, 5g
(c) 200g, 20g, 20g
(d) 200g, 100g, 50g, 20g, 20g, 5g
(e) 100 g, 50 g, 5 g
(f) 500g, 200g, 50g, 10g

76 The Kluless laboratory – *continued*

1 Assuming that the parcels have the weights suggested in the Teacher's Notes, the answers are:
(a) A, D **(b)** B, C, E

2 Assuming that the parcels have the weights suggested in the Teacher's Notes, the weights are:
A 50g B 210g C 140g D 70g E 290g

3 **(a)** Weight of grime: between 130g and 150g
(b) Weight of gunge: between 60g and 70g

4 Answers depend on the children's choice of objects.

5 One box of fungus weighs 21g.
(1 box of mildew weighs 35g.
3 boxes of mildew weigh 105g.
5 boxes of fungus weigh 105g.
so 1 box of fungus weighs 21g (105 ÷ 5).)

77 The pickling room

1 **(a)** 260g **(b)** 260g

2

honey	310g
nettles	540g
vinegar	680g
thistle heads	920g
salt	20g
chilli	140g
dandelion	180g
factor X	260g

78 The pickling room – *continued*

1 hops 1860 g or 1 kg 860 g
elderflowers 480 g
watercress 1140 g or 1 kg 140 g
garlic 420 g
marigold 480 g
spearmint 850 g
basil 1250 g or 1 kg 250 g

2 The answers depend on the weights of the boxes provided by the teacher.

3 Practical work

79 Zantha's Special Fudge

Practical work

80 The Green Hut Gang

1 **(a)** 35 minutes past 9
25 minutes to 10
(b) 55 minutes past 9
5 minutes to 10
(c) 40 minutes past 10
20 minutes to 11
(d) 55 minutes past 10
5 minutes to 11
(e) 35 minutes past 11
25 minutes to 12
(f) 50 minutes past 11
10 minutes to 12
(g) 40 minutes past 12
20 minutes to 1
(h) 45 minutes past 12
15 minutes to 1
(i) 50 minutes past 1
10 minutes to 2

At the cinema 81

1 *Stomper 2* starts just after quarter to five.
The Deep Sea starts just before 20 past 2.
Fright starts just before 25 to 10.
Take-off starts just before 5 past 8.
Crime Squad starts just after 10 to 4.

2 *Stomper 2* starts at 46 minutes past 4.
The Deep Sea starts at 18 minutes past 2.
Fright starts at 34 minutes past 9.
Take-off starts at 3 minutes past 8.
Crime Squad starts at 52 minutes past 3.

3 **(a)** *Mighty Dino:* 23 minutes to 4
(b) *Crusaders:* 13 minutes to 4
(c) *High Jinks:* 28 minutes to 8
(d) *Happy Horace:* 11 minutes to 6
(e) *Scat Cat:* 16 minutes to 12
(f) *Super Duck:* 6 minutes to 8

4 **(a)** 3 minutes to 6
(b) 26 minutes to 6
(c) 22 minutes past 5
(d) 12 minutes past 6

82 Crumble Bar factory

1 (a)

wrapping	23 minutes past 2
arriving	quarter to 1 *or* 15 minutes to 1
pouring	9 minutes past 1
decorating	12 minutes past 2
uniform on	9 minutes to 1
leaving	22 minutes to 4
mixing	26 minutes past 1
packing	7 minutes past 3
cutting	13 minutes to 2

(b) **arriving, uniform on, pouring, mixing, cutting, decorating, wrapping, packing, leaving**

2 (a) 12 minutes past 5
(b) 39 minutes past 5
(c) 57 minutes past 6

83 At the beach

1 (a) 8.30 (b) 1.15 (c) 2.00 (d) 6.45

2 (a) 9.30 (b) 1.15 (c) 2.00 (d) 4.45

3 (a) half past eight
(b) five past ten
(c) twenty to eleven
(d) two o'clock

4 (a) In the shop (b) At the swimming pool
(c) In the café (d) In the snack bar
(e) In the café (f) In the snack bar
(g) In the shop (h) At the swimming pool

At the beach – *continued* 84

1 (a) beautiful baby, best singer
(b) best dancer, best comic, best acrobat, star lookalike

2 best dancer

3 (a) 11.00 am, 11.40 am, 12.20 pm, 1.00 pm, 1.40 pm, 2.20 pm, 6.50 pm, 7.30 pm
(b) 1.00 pm, 1.40 pm, 2.20 pm, 6.50 pm, 7.30 pm

4 9.15 am, 10.15 am, 11.15 am, 12.15 pm, 1.15 pm, 2.15 pm, 3.15 pm

5

12.00	egg and spoon race
12.20 pm	obstacle race
1.00 pm till 1.30 pm	Benny the clown
2.15 pm till 4.00 pm	puppet show

Leisure centre 85

1 (a) Glen spends 15 minutes (b) Karim spends 15 minutes
(c) Mandy spends 25 minutes (d) Matt spends 40 minutes
(e) Roz spends 25 minutes (f) Tessa spends 25 minutes

2

Roz	10 minutes
Glen	45 minutes
Mandy	20 minutes
Matt	15 minutes

3 (a) Glen plays for 35 minutes (b) Karim plays for 40 minutes
(c) Mandy plays for 35 minutes (d) Roz plays for 45 minutes
(e) Matt plays for 40 minutes (f) Matt's friend plays for 50 minutes

86 Leisure centre – *continued*

1

DIVING	Under 15s	2 hours
	Over 15s	3 hours
SWIMMING	Junior	1 hour
	Senior	2 hours
LIFE-SAVING	Bronze medal	3 hours
	Silver medal	2 hours

2 (a) Flumes 1 hour 20 minutes
(b) Turkish baths 1 hour 5 minutes
(c) Diving pool 2 hours 30 minutes
(d) Sauna 1 hour 30 minutes
(e) Learners' pool 1 hour 25 minutes

3 (a) Karim 1 hour 10 minutes
(b) Mandy 1 hour 15 minutes
(c) Glen 1 hour 5 minutes
(d) Matt 25 minutes
(e) Roz 1 hour 10 minutes
(f) Tessa 1 hour 15 minutes

4 'Supergame' lasts 1 hour 10 minutes.
'Cartoon' lasts 15 minutes.
'Star Tour' lasts 35 minutes.

Computer games 87

1 (a) 8 pm (b) 1pm (c) 3.30 pm (d) 1.30 pm (e) 1.15 pm (f) 5.45 pm (g) 2.20 pm (h) 8.40 pm

2 (a) 3.45 pm (b) 10.50 am (c) 6.20 pm (d) 1 pm

3 (a) Karim finishes *Star Trooper* at 5.05 pm
Karim finishes *Lost Princess* at 6.10 pm
Karim finishes *Jungle Drum* at 10.15 am
(b) Roz finishes *Star Trooper* at 12.10 pm
Roz finishes *Lost Princess* at 3.05 pm
Roz finishes *Jungle Drum* at 1.10 pm

Computer games – *continued* 88

1

Player	starts at	plays for	finishes at
Tessa	9.00 am	1 hour	10.00 am
Matt	10.30 am	1 hour	11.30 am
Mandy	11.45 am	2 hours	1.45 pm
Roz	1.50 pm	2 hours	3.50 pm
Glen	4.15 pm	3 hours	7.15 pm

2 (a) Mandy started at 6.05 pm
(b) Matt started at 4.20 pm
(c) Karim started at 2.15 pm
(d) Roz started at 12.25 pm

3 (a) Mandy started at 2.50 pm
(b) Karim started at 9.45 am
(c) Tessa started at 1.55 pm
(d) Roz started at 4.45 pm

89 Green Hut calendar

1 **(a)** Wednesday **(b)** Friday **(c)** Saturday **(d)** Saturday

2 Karim's birthday is Tuesday 21st May.
Glen's birthday is Thursday 16th May.

3 4th May, 11th May, 18th May, 25th May

4 **(a)** One week **(b)** Two weeks
(c) Two weeks **(d)** Three weeks

5 Tuesday, Saturday

6 **(a)** 3.10.52 or 3/10/52 or 03–10–52
(b) 25.8.85 or 25/8/85 or 25–08–85

7 The answers depend on what year it is.

90 Holidays

1 **(a)** 2 weeks
(b) 3 weeks
(c) 3 weeks
(d) 2 weeks

2 30th August

3 Each number in the column is 7 more than the one above it.

4 11th December, 18th December, 25th December

5 26th October

6 **(a)** Saturday 3rd August
(b) Saturday 10th August
(c) Saturday 24th August
(d) Saturday 31st August

Calendar squares 91

1 **(a)** 76
(b) Yes

2 **(a)** Yes. Total is 117.
(b) The method will work for other 3 x 3 squares.

3 Various answers are possible. For example,
(a) Multiply the middle number by 9.
(b) Add top left and bottom right numbers and multiply by 2.

All mixed up 92

1 Weed Wine $\frac{3}{4}$ litre
Nettle Nectar 1 litre or $\frac{4}{4}$ litre
Spruce Syrup $\frac{2}{4}$ litre or $\frac{1}{2}$ litre

2 Practical work

3 **(a)** Practical work
(b) Practical work

4 **(a)** 9 measures **(b)** 6 measures

5 **(a)** Weed wine $\frac{1}{4}$ litre
Juniper juice $1\frac{1}{4}$ litres
Spruce syrup $\frac{3}{4}$ litre
(b) The total volume is $3\frac{1}{4}$ litres.

93 Computer units

1 (a) 9 cm^3 (b) 5 cm^3 (c) 7 cm^3 (d) 7 cm^3 (e) 7 cm^3 (f) 8 cm^3

2 (a) Data Store – 12 cm^3
Thought Control – 16 cm^3
Memory – 15 cm^3

(b) Practical work.

Data Store	shapes **(b)** and **(d)**
Thought Control	shapes **(a)** and **(e)**
Memory	shapes **(c)** and **(f)**

3 Practical work

94 Power packs

1 (a) 8 cm^3 (b) 8 cm^3 (c) 11 cm^3
(d) 10 cm^3 (e) 6 cm^3

2

	(a)	(b)	(c)
Super	10 cm^3	8 cm^3	18 cm^3
Standard	9 cm^3	3 cm^3	12 cm^3
Long life	16 cm^3	8 cm^3	24 cm^3
Powerplus	8 cm^3	19 cm^3	27 cm^3
Triple life	8 cm^3	28 cm^3	36 cm^3

3 Practical work

The stained-glass workshop 95

1, 2

(a)

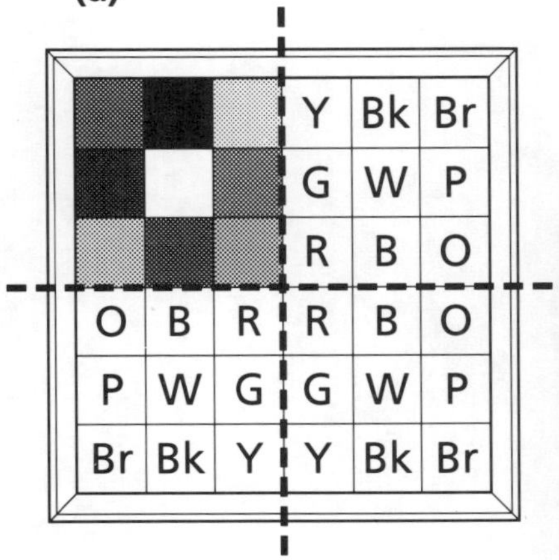

(b)

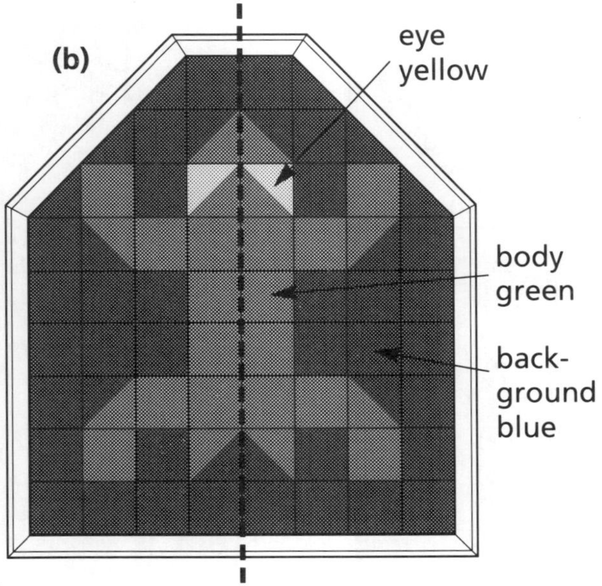

(c)

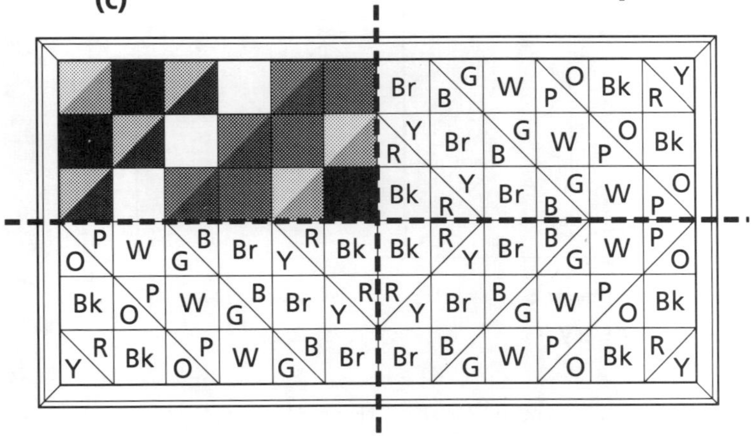

Key

Bk	Black	R	Red
P	Purple	O	Orange
B	Blue	Y	Yellow
Br	Brown	W	White
G	Green		

3 Answers depend on designs chosen.

96 In the frame

1, 2, 3

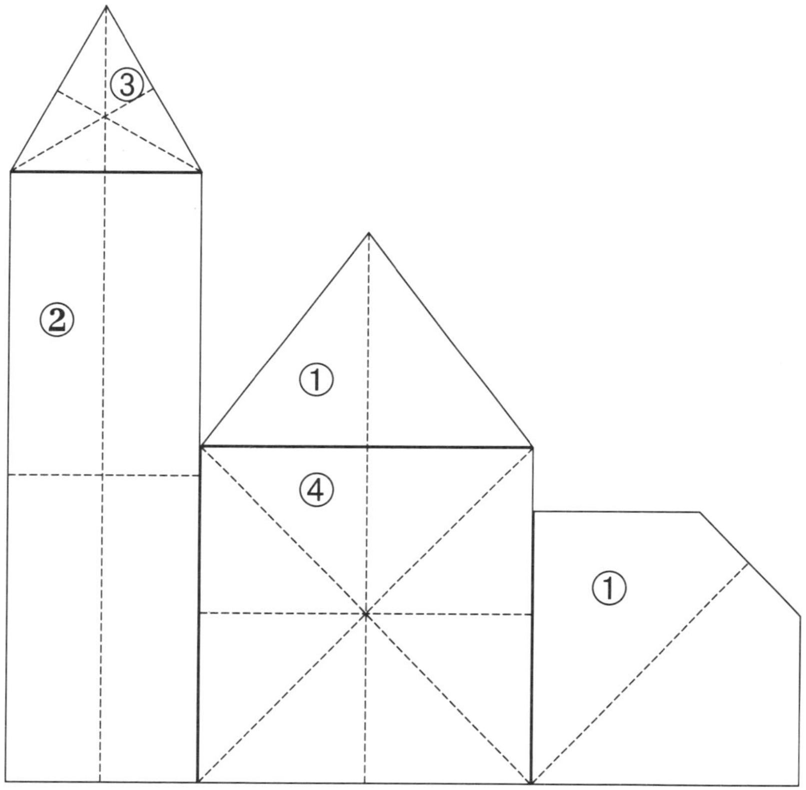

4 **(a), (b), (c)** Practical work
(d) 4 lines of symmetry

5 Practical work

6 **(a)** The answers depend on the child.
(b) Practical work. The correct numbers of 'holes' are:

rectangular cut-outs – 8 holes
curved cut-outs – 8 holes
V-shaped cut-outs – 16 notches

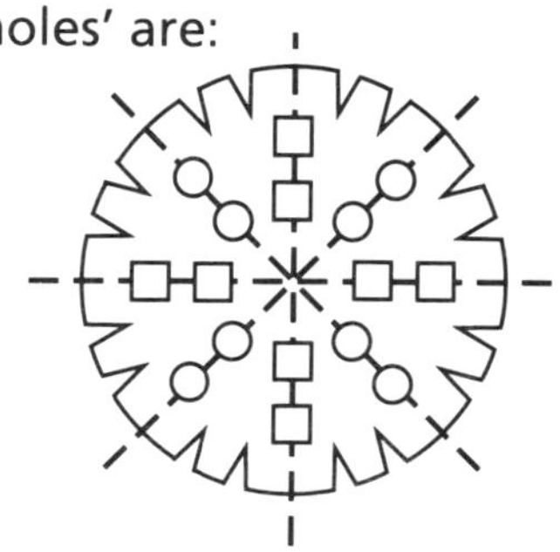

Krazy kites 97

1 Kite **(h)** has no lines of symmetry.

2 **(a)** 2 **(b)** 1 **(c)** 1 **(d)** 3 **(e)** 4
(f) 1 **(g)** 2 **(i)** 5 **(j)** 2

Side by side 98

Practical drawing work. The pattern is as follows:

99 A trinket box

Practical work

100 Nets of a cube

1 (a) Yes, the 6 squares fold to make a cube.

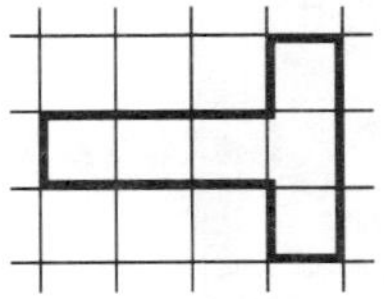

(b) No

(c)

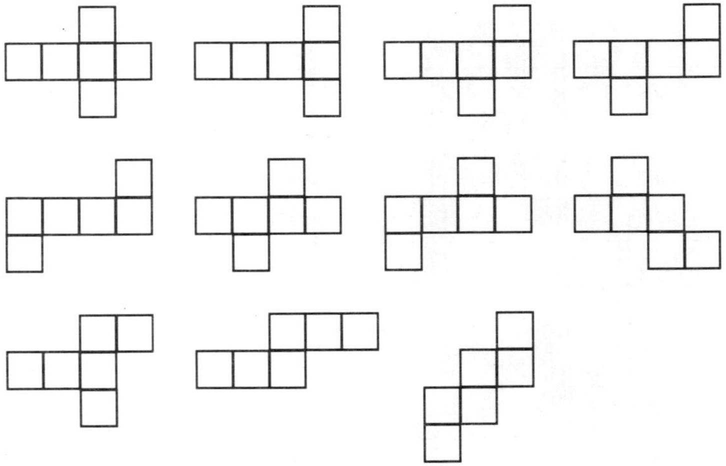

(There are 11 different nets of a cube).

101 Odds and Ends

1 Practical work

2 (a) A variety of nets is possible.
(b) Practical work

3 Practical work

Shapes from triangles 102

1 Practical work

2 (a)  (b) 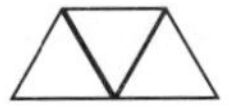

(c) 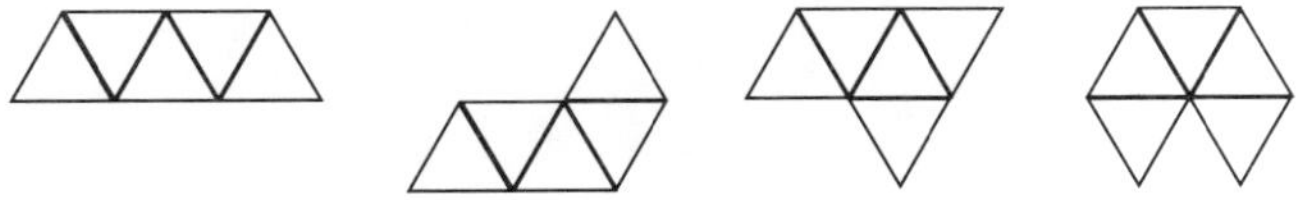

3 Any three of the following shapes:

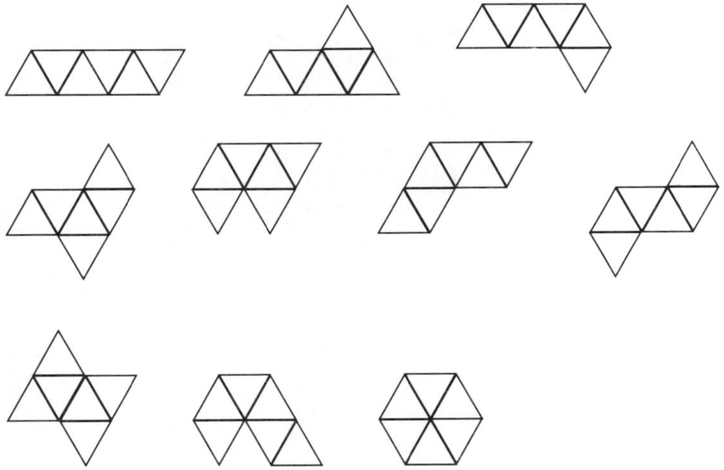

103 Weather machine

1

Right angles	$\frac{1}{2}$	1	$1\frac{1}{2}$	2	$2\frac{1}{2}$	3	$3\frac{1}{2}$	4
Degrees	45°	90°	135°	180°	225°	270°	315°	360°

2 (a) Breezy
(b) Rainy
(c) Sunny
(d) Frosty
(e) Snowy

3 (a) 90° clockwise or 270° anti-clockwise
(b) 45° anti-clockwise or 315° clockwise
(c) 180° clockwise or 180° anti-clockwise
(d) 90° anti-clockwise or 270° clockwise
(e) 135° clockwise or 225° anti-clockwise
(f) 90° anti-clockwise or 270° clockwise
(g) 135° clockwise or 225° anti-clockwise
(h) 90° clockwise or 270° anti-clockwise

Fishing fleet 104

1 (a) Mull (b) Coll (c) Tiree
(d) Barra (e) Arran (f) Islay

2 (a) East (b) Northwest
(c) Southeast (d) West
(e) Southwest (f) South

3

Hamish faces	he turns through	he now faces
Skye	90° clockwise	Islay
Arran	180° anti-clockwise	Jura
Tiree	135° clockwise	Skye
Jura	360° anti-clockwise	Jura
Coll	90° anti-clockwise	Islay
Arran	45° clockwise	Skye
Jura	90° clockwise	Tiree
Barra	135° anti-clockwise	Mull
Jura	135° anti-clockwise	Skye

Lisa's Robot 105

1 **I** FD 4
S FD 1, BK 1, RT 90, FD 2, LT 90, FD 2, LT 90, FD 2, RT 90, FD 2, RT 90, FD 2, RT 90, FD 1
A FD 4, RT 90, FD 2, RT 90, FD 2, RT 90, FD 2, BK 2, LT 90, FD 2
Other sets of commands are possible.

2 Her brother's name is PETE.

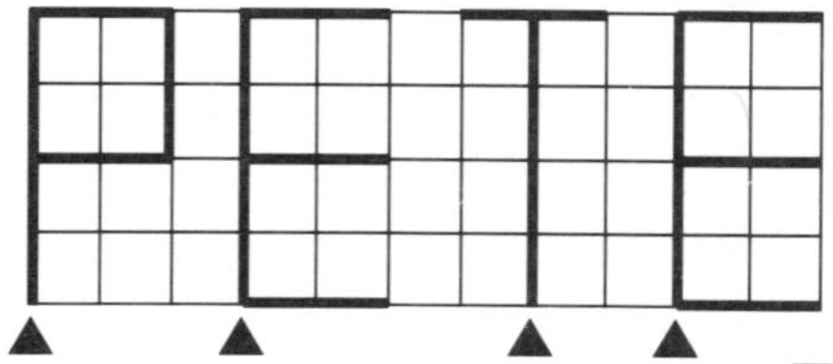

3 FD 3, RT 90, FD 1, RT 90, FD 2, RT 90, FD 2, RT 90, FD 1, RT 90, FD 3, RT 90, FD 1, RT 90, FD 1, LT 90, FD 1, RT 90, FD 1
The answer depends on the starting point.

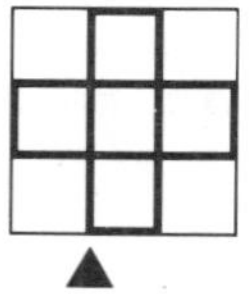

106 Newspaper round

1 FD 2, LT 90, FD 8, LT 90, FD 3

2 **(a)** Rose Cottage
(b) Smallburn Inn

3 Hillend Farm and Mystery Manor

4 **(a)** Hillend Farm FD 9, LT 90, FD 3, RT 90, FD 12
Torwood Tower FD 2, LT 90, FD 9, RT 90, FD 4, LT 90, FD 5
There are other correct routes which use the 'fewest possible' commands.
(b) The answer depends on the answers to part **(a)**.
The route to Hillend Farm should use fewer commands.

5 One possible answer is:
FD 11, RT 90, FD 10, BK 5, LT 90, FD 11, BK 13, FD 3, LT 90, FD 9, BK 2, RT 90, FD 2, RT 90, FD 1, LT 90, FD 2, BK 2, LT 90, FD 1, LT 90, FD 2, LT 90, FD 2, RT 90, FD 5, RT 90, FD 6, BK 6, LT 90, FD 7.
Other sets of 'fewest commands' are possible. Some children may not wish to use the BK command and will find longer routes.

6 It starts at Mystery Manor.

107 Cora's computer

1 **(a)** a spaceman **(b)** a rocket
(c) the moon **(d)** stars

2 **(a)** C1 **(b)** B2

3 **(a)** traffic cones **(b)** a caravan **(c)** traffic lights
(d) road works **(e)** trees

4 **(a)** 2,4 **(b)** 7,1 **(c)** 1,2 **(d)** 3,1

Cora's computer *– continued* 108

1 **(a)** **WELL DONE**
YOU ARE IN
THE HALL OF FAME
(b) Answer depends on the child.

2 **(a)**, **(b)** and **(c)**

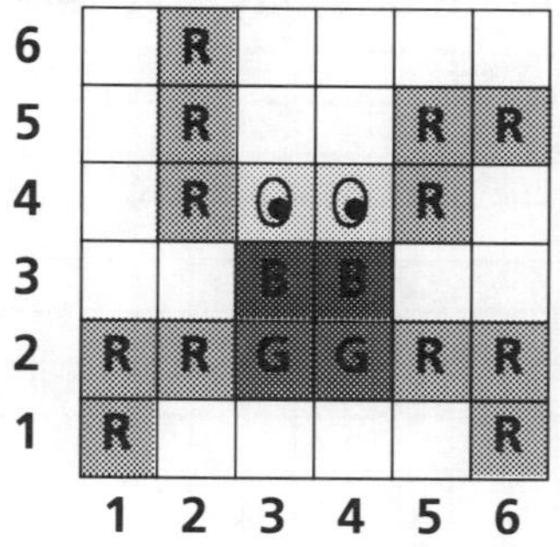

(d) Answer depends on the child's choice.

Circles 109

Practical drawing work

Circles *– continued* 110

Practical drawing work

111 Atholl Wood

1 (a) 32 (b) 17 (c) 29

2 (a) 20 (b) 13 (c) 8

3 The total number of insects found was 161.

4 (a)

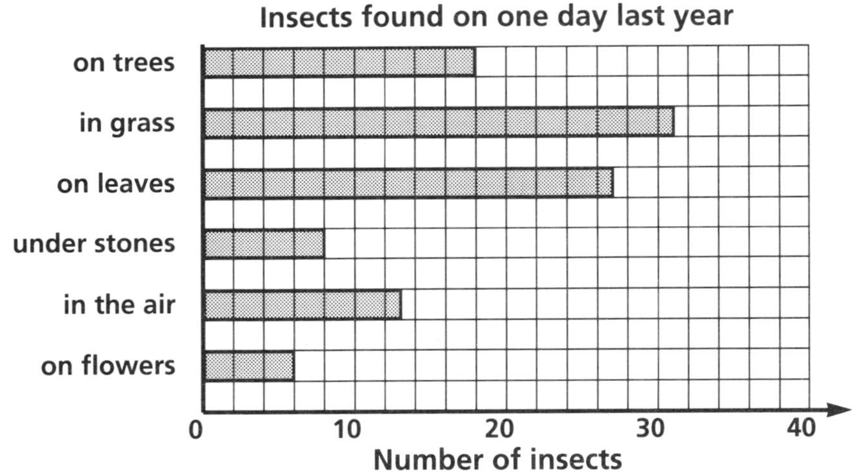

(b) The number of insects found on flowers has changed most.
Possible answers include:
- late flowering due to the weather
- survey made at a different time of day or year.

112 Atholl Wood *– continued*

1 Oak 24, beech 42, birch 40, elm 34

2 140

3 Oak 18, beech 0, birch 2, elm 8
There are other possible correct answers.

4 (a) 30 (b) Between 40 and 50

5 (a) 9 – 11 am, 11 am – 1 pm (b) 7 – 9 am, 1 – 3 pm, 5 – 7 pm

6 1 – 3 pm

113 Summer visitors

1 (a)

swallows	35
warblers	22
swifts	28
redstarts	45
flycatchers	10

(b) The total number of birds was 140.

2

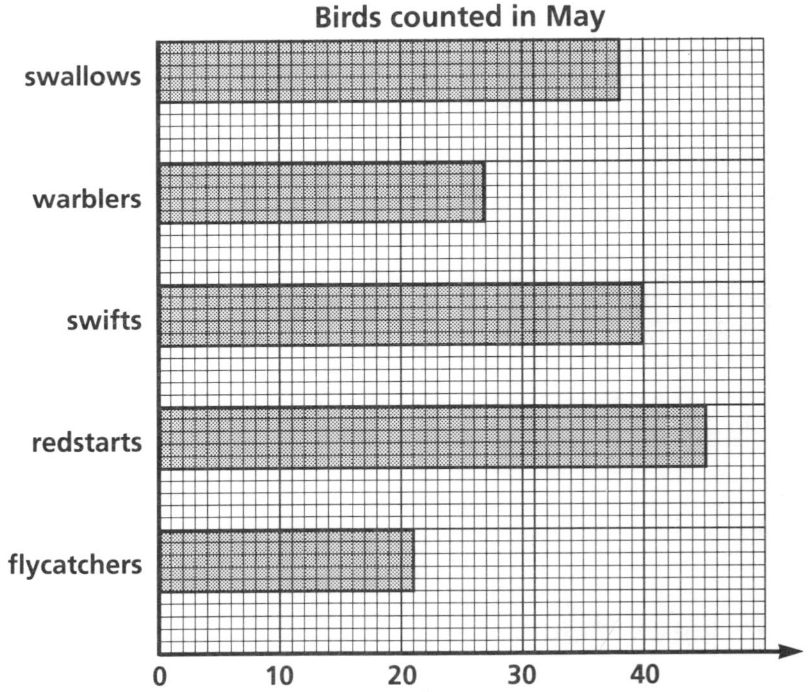

3 (a) swallows by 3
warblers by 5
swifts by 12
flycatchers by 11

(b) A possible answer would be that more of these birds arrived from other countries in April and May.
The redstarts had probably all arrived by March.

(c) 31

114 Summer visitors – *continued*

1 (a) 50 came from France
66 came from Spain
32 came from Italy
48 came from Portugal
64 came from Turkey
(b) The total number of birds is 260.
(c) No. Only 114 came from Spain and Portugal.

2

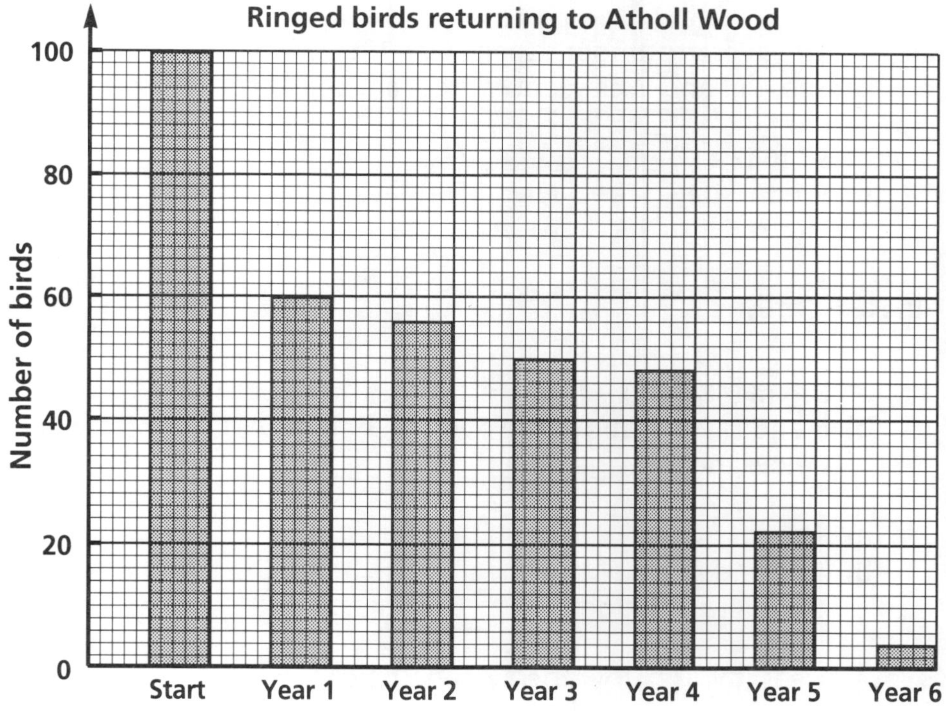

3 (a) 40 ringed birds did not return.
(b) A possible reason is the danger of immigration for young birds.
(c) A likely reason is that the birds are coming to the end of their lives, as well as the danger of immigration for old birds.

Animals in Atholl Wood 115

1 (a) 13 deer, 28 squirrels, 52 rabbits
(b) 93 animals altogether

2 (6 deer, 39 squirrels, 22 rabbits – 67 animals altogether)
They saw 26 fewer animals.

3

	Fern Hill	Berry Glade	Mill Copse	Total
Deer	9	6	13	28
Squirrels	36	39	28	103
Rabbits	72	22	52	146
Total	117	67	93	277

Would you touch...? 116

All answers depend on the children's own surveys.

Yellow group's insect survey 117

1 It took place in Atholl Wood, on 6 July, between 6.00 am and 11.00 pm.

2 It lasted for 17 hours.

3 The total number of insects surveyed was 176.

4 (a) Yes (108 out of 176 had 2 colours.)
(b) Yes (48 out of 176 were ladybirds.)

5 violet ground beetle, ladybird
hover-fly, lacewing

6 Possible answers include:
– it is about $1\frac{1}{2}$ cm long
– it is orange and black.

118 Yellow group's insect survey – *continued*

1

Insects	Week 1	Week 2	Week 3	Total
ladybirds	48	46	51	145
hover-flies	44	49	43	136
Total	92	95	94	281

2 **(a)** 145
(b) 5
(c) Week 2
(d) Week 1 and week 3

3

Insects	Week 1	Week 2	Week 3	Total
ladybirds	48	51	51	150
hover-flies	44	49	43	136
Total	92	100	94	286

119 Atholl Wood averages

1 **(a)** Seb raised £7
Bill raised £5
Pam raised £4
Wes raised £6
Li raised £5
Jan raised £9
(b) The total raised is £36
(c) £6
(d) Wes
(e) Seb and Jan raised more, Bill, Pam and Li raised less.

2 **(a)** Sketching flowers **(F)** 15 minutes
Collecting leaves **(L)** 35 minutes
Counting birds **(B)** 10 minutes
Planting trees **(T)** 40 minutes
(b) 25 minutes
(c) No
(d) Collecting leaves and planting trees took more time, sketching flowers and counting birds took less time.

120 Atholl Wood averages – *continued*

1 **(a)** Seb spent 70p
Bill spent 75p
Pam spent 55p
Wes spent 80p
Li spent 45p
Jan spent 65p
(b) The total amount spent was £3·90
(c) 65p

2 **(a)** The average amount spent was 72p. (360 ÷ 5)
(b) Seb, Bill and Wes spent more, Pam and Li spent less.

3 **(a)** 91 (637 ÷ 7)
(b) Wednesday, Saturday and Sunday

121 Investigations

1 **(a)** 81 cm (486 ÷ 6)
(b) B and D were above the average height, A, C, E and F were below the average height.

2 **(a)** 117 cm
(b) A, B and D are above the average height, C, E and F are below the average height.

3 Last year it was below the average height, this year it is above.

4 The answers depend on the children's surveys.

122 Is it likely?

1 certain

2 unlikely

3 impossible

4 likely or very likely

5 likely or very likely

6 very unlikely

7 very unlikely

8 likely or very likely

123 More or less likely

1 A is more likely

2 C is less likely

3 **(a)** orange **(b)** green

4 **(a)** blue
(b) green

5 5, 6 or 7 badges should be coloured blue.

Shapes within shapes 124

1 **(a)**

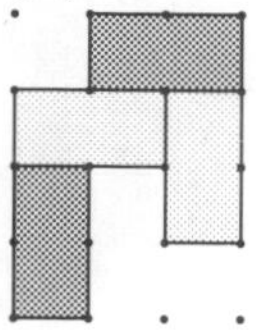

(b)

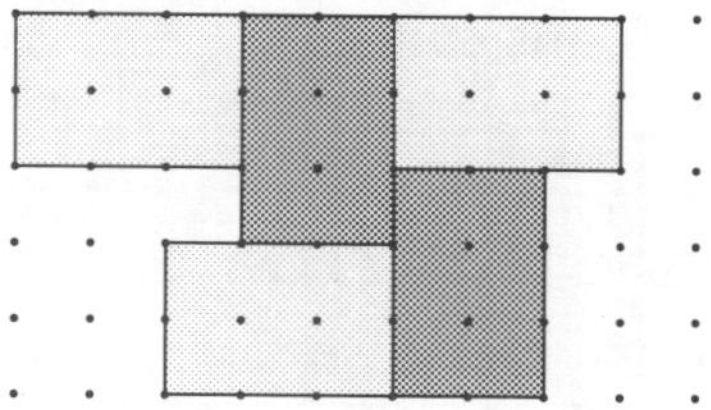

(c)

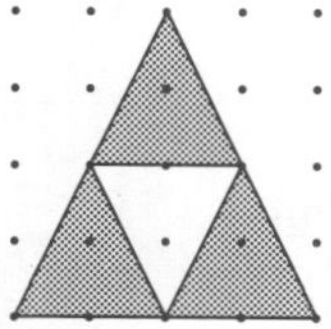

(d)

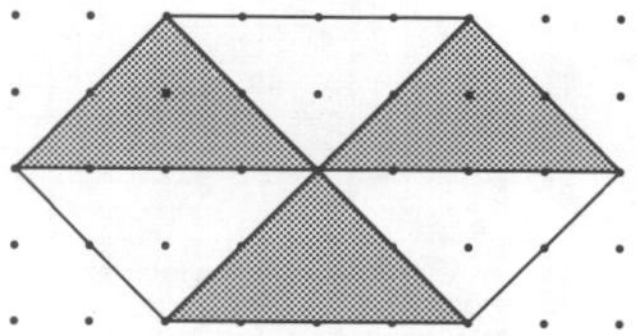

2 **(a)** Possible answers include:

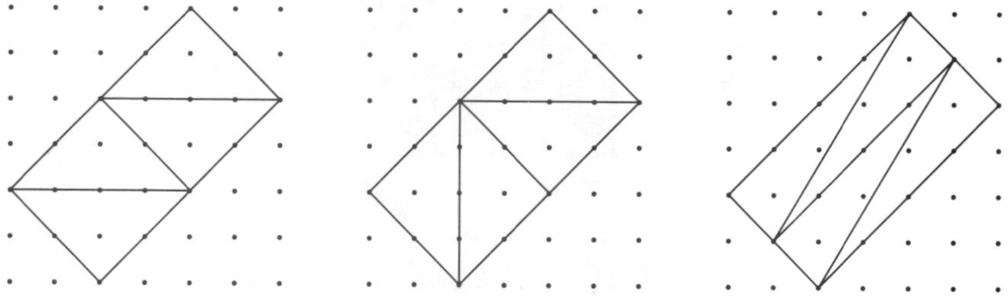

(b) Possible answers include:

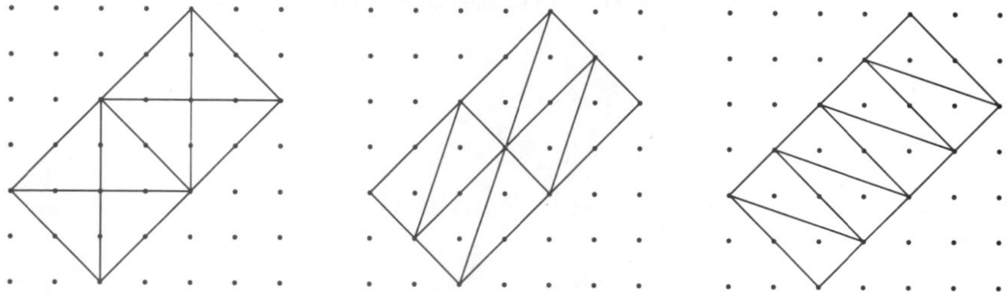

125 Recycling

1 (a) No

(b)

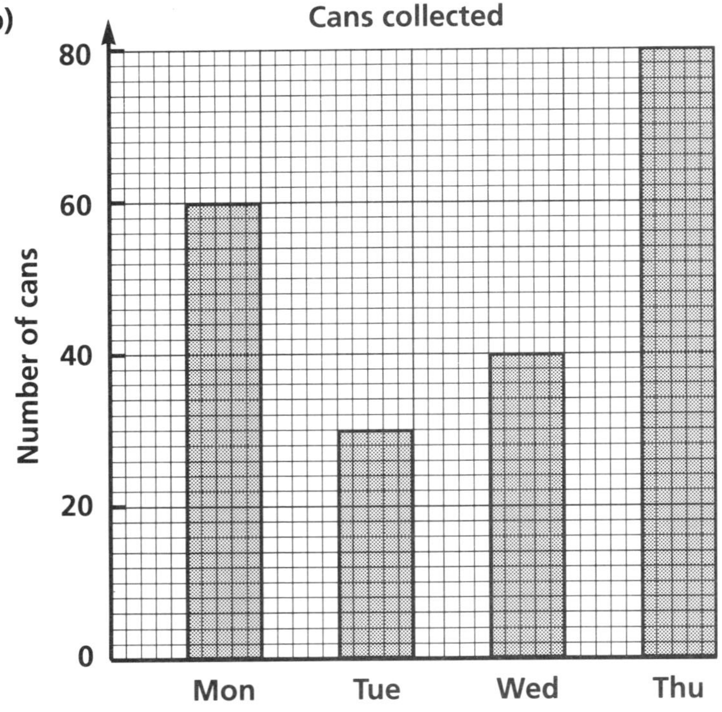

(c) The best day was Thursday, the worst day was Tuesday.

(d) The vertical scales of the two graphs are different.

Recycling – *continued* 125

2 (a) No

(b)

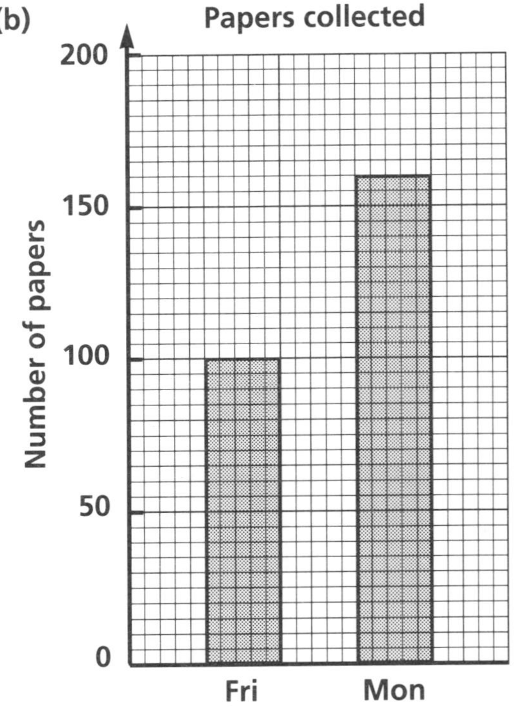

(c) The vertical scale starts at '**40**' instead of '**0**'.

1 Mental subtraction of U from TU

The map

1 58 − 5 = 53 29 − 3 = 26

73 − 10 = 63 73 − 9 = 64 96 − 10 = 86 96 − 9 = 87

85 − 7 = is the same as 85 − 5 − 2

= 80 − 2 = 78

2 50 − 4 = 46 30 − 3 = 27 90 − 5 = 85 92 − 7 = 85

84 − 9 = 75 25 − 8 = 17 51 − 2 = 49 44 − 8 = 36

71 − 6 = 65 88 − 6 = 82 94 − 7 = 87 72 − 5 = 67

52 − 9 = 43 95 − 7 = 88 41 − 4 = 37 86 − 8 = 78

Problem solving

3 Complete.

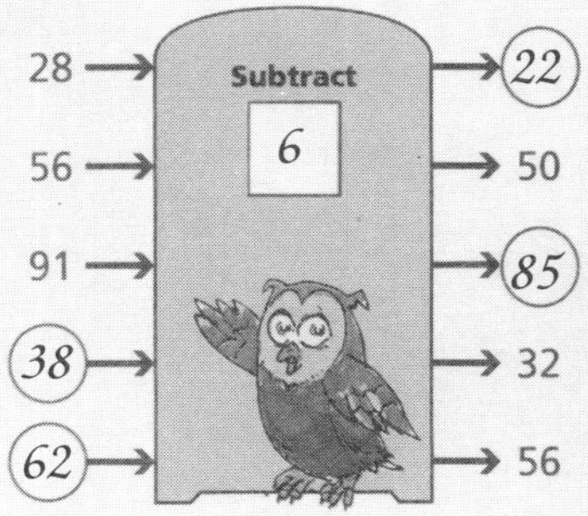

4 Colour five more pairs of numbers whose difference is 65.

9	70	5	7	10
82	10	93	4	75
3	68	5	0	64
49	7	60	65	27
10	1	2	38	6
55	66	7	74	9

5 Make 36 by adding or subtracting.
Use any numbers you like.

Possible answers are:

136−100 → 36

44 − 10 + 2 → 36

40−4 → 36

30+6 → 36

7+9+20 → 36

26+10 → 36

There are many possible answers.

Go to Textbook page 3.

2 Numbers to 9999: place value

In the Emerald Forest

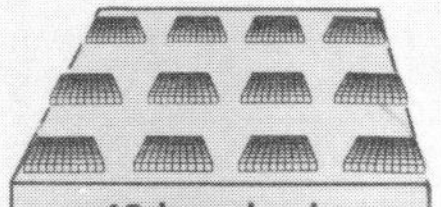

12 hundreds →

Thousands	Hundreds	Tens	Units
1	2	0	0

1 14 hundreds = 1 thousand + 4 hundreds = 1400

18 hundreds = 1 thousand + 8 hundreds = 1800

20 hundreds = 2 thousands + 0 hundreds = 2000

35 hundreds = 3 thousands + 5 hundreds = 3500

2 4600 = 4 thousands + 6 hundreds + 0 tens + 0 units

5790 = 5 thousands + 7 hundreds + 9 tens + 0 units

6358 = 6 thousands + 3 hundreds + 5 tens + 8 units

6079 = 6 thousands + 0 hundreds + 7 tens + 9 units

3 (a) 3000 = 3 thousands = 30 hundreds

(b) 5000 = 5 thousands = 50 hundreds

(c) 5700 = 57 hundreds (d) 8600 = 86 hundreds

3 Numbers to 9999: place value

Tree house

1638	→	1000	+	600	+	30	+	8
2917	→	*2000*	+	*900*	+	*10*	+	*7*
3076	→	*3000*	+	*70*	+	*6*		
6217	→	6000	+	200	+	10	+	7
5040	→	5000	+	40				

4263	→	four thousand, two hundred and sixty-three
5927	→	*five thousand, nine hundred and twenty-seven*
6108	→	*six thousand one hundred and eight*
7084	→	seven thousand and eighty-four
9909	→	nine thousand, nine hundred and nine

	Number after
3562	*3563*
4000	*4001*
3299	*3300*
5099	*5100*

Number before	
2385	2386
2999	3000
4299	4300
5009	5010

The 3 means 3 tens.

2 5 ③ 8 →	3 tens
3 ⑦ 1 4 →	*7 hundreds*
6 0 2 ⑤ →	*5 units*
7 9 ⓪ 3 →	*0 tens*
⑧ 1 1 2 →	*8 thousands*

Go to Textbook page 7.

R1

4 Place value, addition and subtraction: consolidation

Explorers' log

1 Use the pictures to complete this log.

Our adventure began in the cave where we found that one dragon was *2836* kg heavier than the other. The owl gave us a map. Tony walked *44* m from Golden Pond to Gem Leaf. Kelvin and Lisa collected *421* pearls in Pearl Garden. The purple box in the pyramid had the symbols *Ⴤ⊲Φ* on it. We visited Emerald Forest where *7800* tree people lived. Kelvin saw three castles. *1979* Millitrogs lived there. After the party they gave us *3056* milligums to bring home.

2674
357
19
+ 6
3056

455
596
+ 928
1979

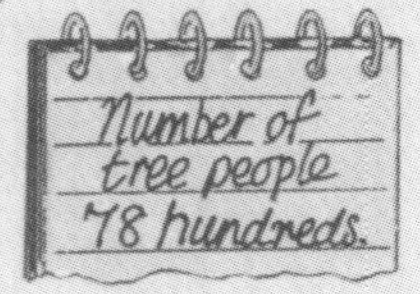

Subtract 4868 from 5305.

5305
−4868
437

1	♀		5	⅄
3	⊲		7	Φ
4	Ⴤ		8	ʃ

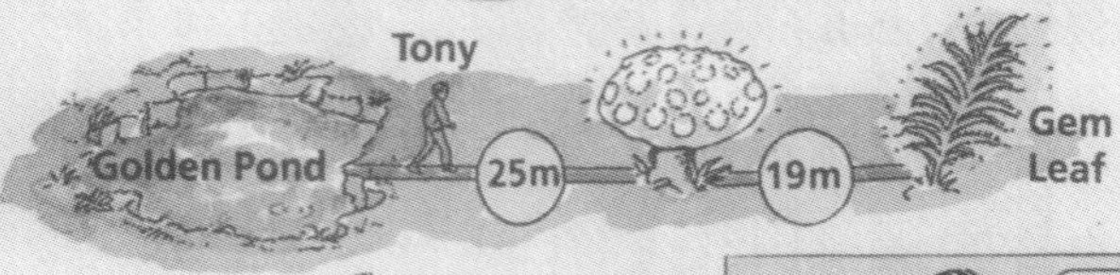

5000
−2164
2836

237
+ 184
421

Ask your teacher what to do next.

5 Multiplication: tables facts

Page count

Steve has made a table to find the number of pages needed for copies of different magazines.

1 **Multiply** to complete Steve's table.

Pages in one magazine	Number of magazines								
	2	3	4	5	6	7	8	9	10
3	6	9	12	15	18	21	24	27	30
4	8	12	16	20	24	28	32	36	40
5	10	15	20	25	30	35	40	45	50
6	12	18	24	30	36	42	48	54	60
7	14	21	28	35	42	49	56	63	70
8	16	24	32	40	48	56	64	72	80
9	18	27	36	45	54	63	72	81	90
10	20	30	40	50	60	70	80	90	100

2 Look along the row for 3 pages.
What number is **added** each time to make the pattern? 3

3 What number is **added** to make the pattern in the row for

4 pages 4 7 pages 7 10 pages? 10

4 (a) Steve extends his table by **adding**. Complete:

Pages in one magazine	Number of magazines										
	10	11	12	13	14	15	16	17	18	19	20
3	30	33	36	39	42	45	48	51	54	57	60
4	40	44	48	52	56	60	64	68	72	76	80
5	50	55	60	65	70	75	80	85	90	95	100
6	60	66	72	78	84	90	96	102	108	114	120
7	70	77	84	91	98	105	112	119	126	133	140

(b) Check the column for 19 magazines by **multiplying**.

Go to Textbook page 19.

6 Multiplication: Th HTU by 2 to 9

Number fun from *Galaxy*

Try these problems from the 'Number fun' page in *Galaxy* magazine.

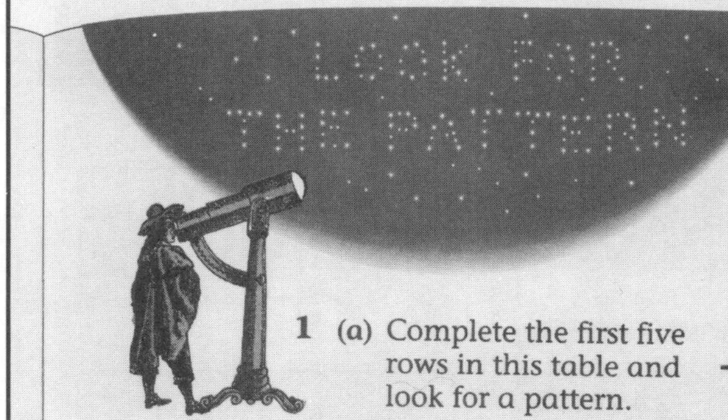

1 (a) Complete the first five rows in this table and look for a pattern.

(b) **Use the pattern** to complete the rest of the table.

(c) Check your answers for row 6 to row 9.

1 × 1089 =	1	0	8	9
2 × 1089 =	2	1	7	8
3 × 1089 =	3	2	6	7
4 × 1089 =	4	3	5	6
5 × 1089 =	5	4	4	5
6 × 1089 =	6	5	3	4
7 × 1089 =	7	6	2	3
8 × 1089 =	8	7	1	2
9 × 1089 =	9	8	0	1

2 Here is **Code 1066** from a famous detective's *Book of Codes*. It shows how to change letters into numbers.

(a) Use the **number machine** to complete **Code 1066**.

Letter	Number	Multiplied by 1066
R	1	1066
X	2	2132
S	3	3198
A	4	4264
D	5	5330
M	6	6396
F	7	7462
E	8	8528
O	9	9594

(b) Use **Code 1066** to find:

- **the detective's name**

6396 9594 1066 3198 8528
M O R S E

- **the town where he works.**

9594 2132 7462 9594 1066 5330
O X F O R D

Go to Textbook page 25.

7 Time: durations, consolidation

The gang are planning their day at Wonderpark.

Adventure Ride $1\frac{1}{2}$ hours	Video Fun 20 minutes	Tunnel Twister 50 minutes	Dino Walk 45 minutes	River Rapids 35 minutes

1 Complete their timetable for all 5 activities.

Start	Activity	Finish
9 am	Adventure Ride	*10.30 am*
10.30 am	Tunnel Twister	*11.20 am*
11.20 am	Video Fun	*11.40 am*
11.40 am	River Rapids	*12.15 pm*
12.15 pm	Dino Walk	*1.00 pm*

Problem solving

2 Complete their **afternoon** timetable for all 5 activities.

Start	Activity	Finish
2 pm	Dino Walk	*2.45 pm*
2.45 pm	Tunnel Twister	*3.35 pm*
3.35 pm	*River Rapids*	*4.10 pm*
4.10 pm	Adventure Ride	*5.40 pm*
5.40 pm	*Video Fun*	*6.00 pm*

Ask your teacher what to do next.

8 Division: HTU ÷ 2, 3, 4, 5 using material

Streamers

Streamers for the Carnival come in boxes containing 100 or 10 or 1.

Use hundreds, tens and units to represent the boxes.

1 Share the 324 streamers equally between 2 floats.

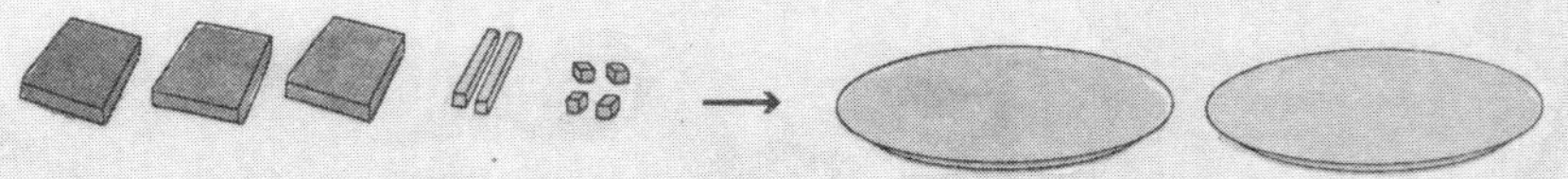

Share the 3 hundreds.

Exchange 1 hundred for 10 tens.

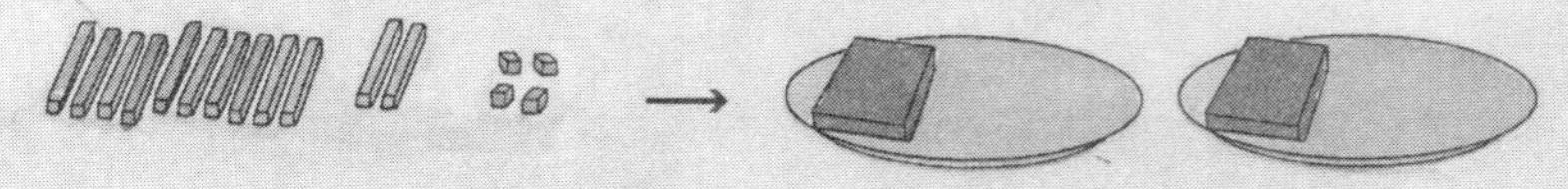

Share the 12 tens.
Share the 4 units.
There are 162 streamers for each float.

Use material to divide.

2 228 ÷ 2 = *114* 260 ÷ 2 = *130* 312 ÷ 3 = *104* 306 ÷ 3 = *102*

254 ÷ 2 = *127* 338 ÷ 3 = *112 r 2* 416 ÷ 4 = *104* 453 ÷ 4 = *113 r 1*

3 $3\overline{)423}$ = *141* $4\overline{)128}$ = *32* $5\overline{)157}$ = *31 r 2* $2\overline{)156}$ = *78*

$5\overline{)135}$ = *27* $4\overline{)117}$ = *29 r 1* $3\overline{)316}$ = *105 r 1* $2\overline{)339}$ = *169 r 1*

Problem solving

4 These streamers have already been shared.

Complete: $3\overline{)410}$ = *136 r2*

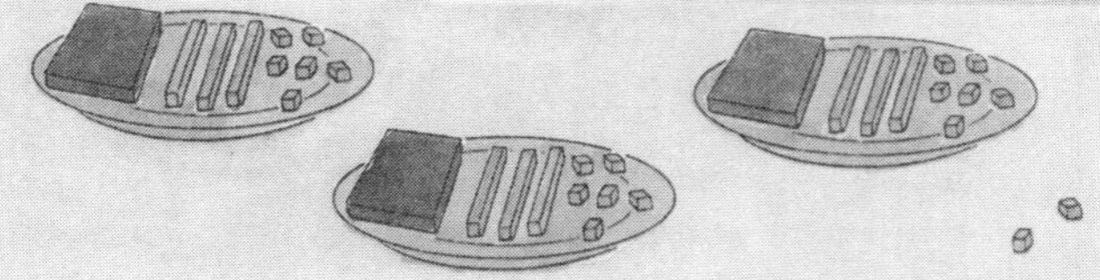

Go to Textbook page 36.

9 Division: consolidation

Carnival message

Q 336	E 83	N 124	J 92	Z 392	O 7
Y 224	B 11	T 59	H 101	P 165	E 83
I 150	F 8	W 109	U 30	Z 392	N 124
A 14	N 124	C 26	D 94	B 11	G 87
X 196	A 14	M 6	R 57	E 83	S 105

1 Find each answer. Colour **all** the boxes that have this answer.

64 ÷ 8 = 8 300 ÷ 10 = 30 54 ÷ 9 = 6

7⟌98 = 14 2⟌166 = 83 4⟌496 = 124 10⟌870 = 87

5⟌505 = 101 3⟌672 = 224 6⟌354 = 59 9⟌828 = 92

56 divided by 8 = 7

Share 630 among 6.
How many each?

6⟌630 = 105 each

Sort 658 into groups of 7.
How many groups?

7⟌658 = 94 groups

2 Use the coloured squares to find the hidden message.

E N J O Y / T H E / F U N / A N D / G A M E S

10 Division: money, consolidation

Carnival Snacks

1 Use the bill.
Find the price of **one** of each item.
Complete each label.

Carnival Snacks BILL

8 burgers	£8·48
10 colas	£6·50
6 oranges	£2·34
7 pizzas	£8·61
9 crisps	£3·06
5 sweets	£1·50
9 toffee apples	£7·47

31	32	33	34	35	36
37	38	39	40	41	42
43	44	45	46	47	48
49	50	51	52	53	54
55	56	57	58	59	60

2 Colour numbers that have

(a) no remainder when divided by 8, ⟶ red

(b) a remainder of 1 when divided by 7, ⟶ blue

(c) a remainder of 4 when divided by 5, ⟶ green

Go to Textbook page 43.

11 Fractions: equivalence

Carnival Colour

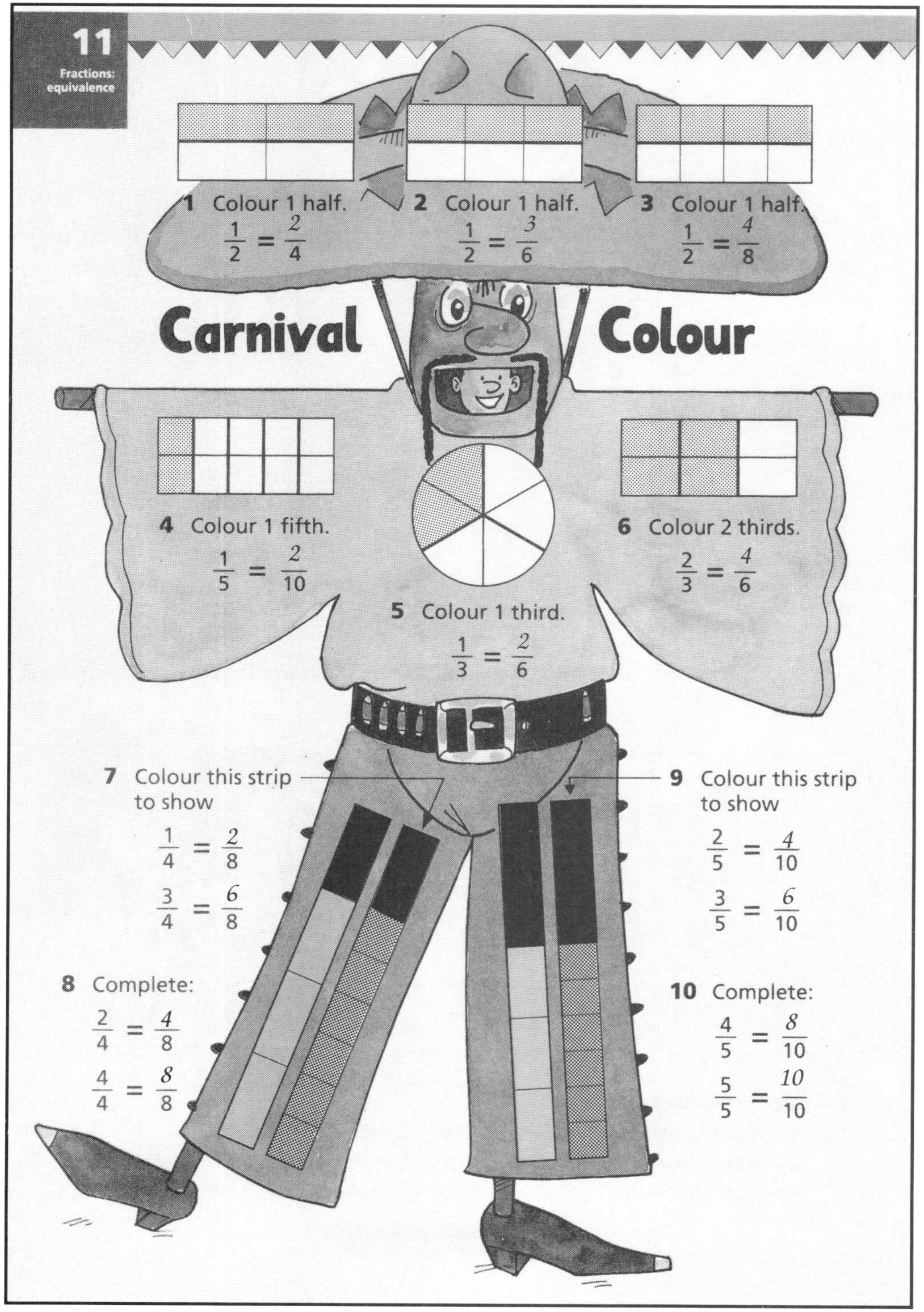

1 Colour 1 half.
$\frac{1}{2} = \frac{2}{4}$

2 Colour 1 half.
$\frac{1}{2} = \frac{3}{6}$

3 Colour 1 half.
$\frac{1}{2} = \frac{4}{8}$

4 Colour 1 fifth.
$\frac{1}{5} = \frac{2}{10}$

5 Colour 1 third.
$\frac{1}{3} = \frac{2}{6}$

6 Colour 2 thirds.
$\frac{2}{3} = \frac{4}{6}$

7 Colour this strip to show
$\frac{1}{4} = \frac{2}{8}$
$\frac{3}{4} = \frac{6}{8}$

8 Complete:
$\frac{2}{4} = \frac{4}{8}$
$\frac{4}{4} = \frac{8}{8}$

9 Colour this strip to show
$\frac{2}{5} = \frac{4}{10}$
$\frac{3}{5} = \frac{6}{10}$

10 Complete:
$\frac{4}{5} = \frac{8}{10}$
$\frac{5}{5} = \frac{10}{10}$

12 Fractions: equivalence

Bouncy castle

1 Colour to show
$\frac{2}{4} = \frac{1}{2}$

2 Colour to show
$\frac{4}{8} = \frac{1}{2}$

3 Colour to show
$\frac{5}{10} = \frac{1}{2}$

4 Colour to show
$\frac{2}{8} = \frac{1}{4}$
$\frac{6}{8} = \frac{3}{4}$

1 whole									
$\frac{1}{2}$					$\frac{1}{2}$				
$\frac{1}{5}$		$\frac{1}{5}$		$\frac{1}{5}$		$\frac{1}{5}$		$\frac{1}{5}$	
$\frac{1}{10}$	$\frac{1}{10}$	$\frac{1}{10}$	$\frac{1}{10}$	$\frac{1}{10}$	$\frac{1}{10}$	$\frac{1}{10}$	$\frac{1}{10}$	$\frac{1}{10}$	$\frac{1}{10}$

5 Use the diagram to help you.

$\frac{2}{10} = \frac{1}{5}$ $\frac{4}{10} = \frac{2}{5}$ $\frac{6}{10} = \frac{3}{5}$ $\frac{5}{10} = \frac{1}{2}$ $\frac{8}{10} = \frac{4}{5}$ $\frac{2}{2} = \frac{10}{10}$

Problem solving

6 Find different pairs of numbers for □ and △.

$\frac{1}{2} = \frac{2}{4}$ $\frac{1}{3} = \frac{2}{6}$ $\frac{1}{5} = \frac{2}{10}$

Ask your teacher what to do next.

There are other correct pairs.

R18

13 Decimals: notation

Pennants

0·5 ($\frac{5}{10}$ or $\frac{1}{2}$) of this pennant design is red. ⟶

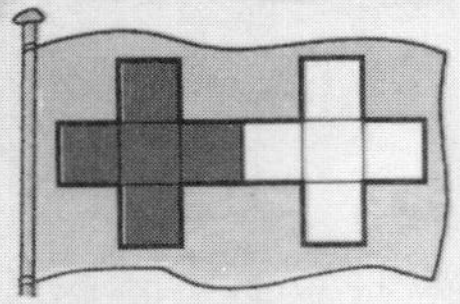

1 Colour each design to show the decimal fraction.

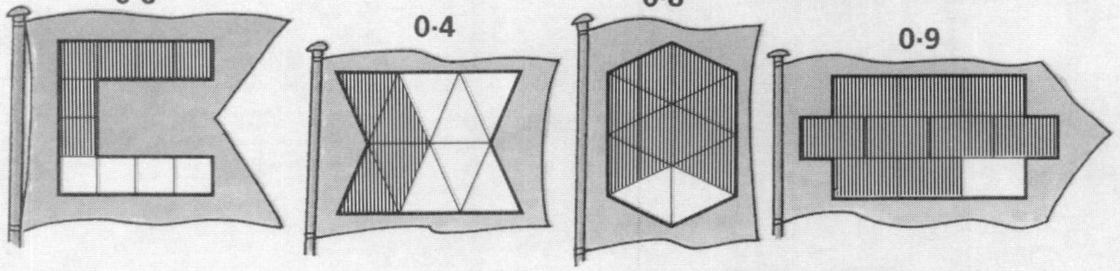

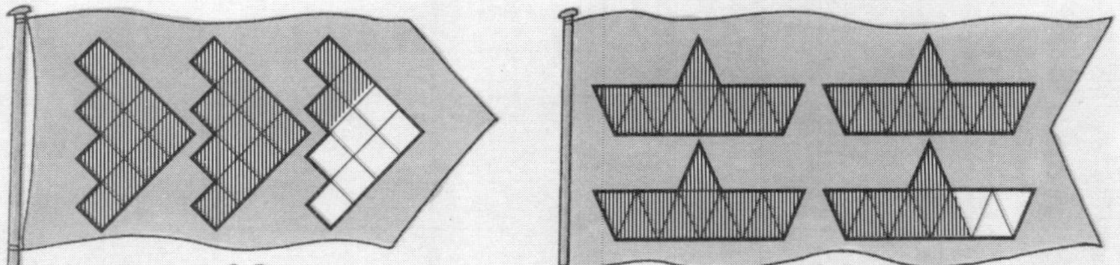

Other shadings are possible.

2 The water level changes during the year.

(a) The arrow shows the January level as **3·3 metres**. Complete the other levels.

(b) Draw arrows to show these levels

April 2·5 m October 2·1 m
June 0·9 m December 3·0 m.

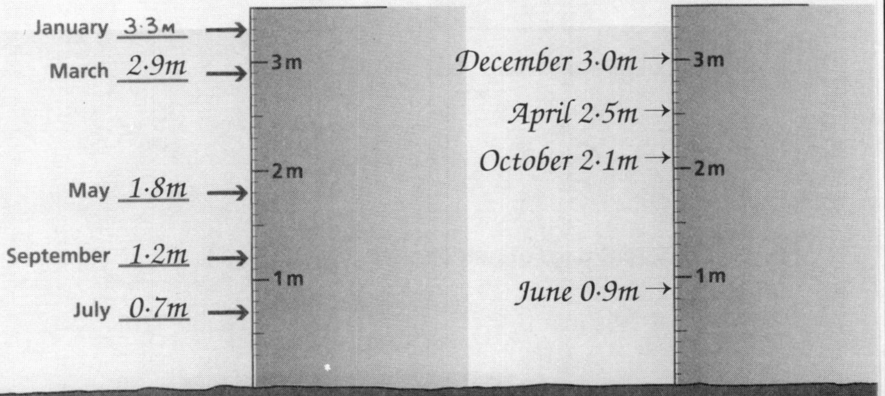

R19

Go to Textbook page 53.

14 Decimals: addition, no exchange

Patches

1 Colour 2 tenths of the sail patch red.
Colour 5 tenths of the sail patch blue.

(a) What fraction of the patch have you coloured altogether? *0·7*

(b) Complete:

  0·2
+ 0·5
0·7

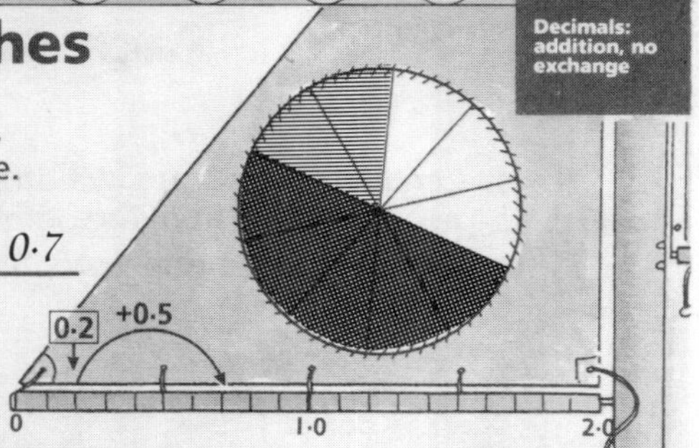

2 (a) Colour red ⟶ 0·1
blue ⟶ 0·3
green ⟶ 0·4

(b) Complete:

  0·1
  0·3
+ 0·4
0·8

3 Find mentally:

(a) 0·2 + 0·4 = *0·6* (b) 0·4 + 0·3 = *0·7* (c) 0·7 + 0·2 = *0·9*

(d) 0·3 + 0·5 = *0·8* (e) 0·5 + 0·1 + 0·3 = *0·9* (f) 0·2 + 0·4 + 0·3 = *0·9*

Vijay uses 2 pieces of wood to patch the deck.
The pieces are 1·5 metres and 2·4 metres long.

Add the tenths. 5 and 4 is 9 tenths.
Add the units. 1 and 2 is 3 units.

  2·4 m
+ 1·5 m
  3·9 m

Altogether he uses **3·9 metres.**

4 Add these lengths of wood.

(a) 1·4 m + 2·3 m = *3·7m*
(b) 3·6 m + 4·2 m = *7·8m*
(c) 7·4 m + 1·5 m = *8·9m*
(d) 6·0 m + 0·4 m = *6·4m*
(e) 0·7 m + 5·2 m = *5·9m*
(f) 6·3 m + 1·5 m = *7·8m*

5 Find

(a) 26·4 + 12·3 = *38·7*
(b) 37·1 + 21·6 = *58·7*
(c) 54·2 + 30·0 = *84·2*
(d) 14·5 + 83·4 = *97·9*
(e) 50·4 + 6·1 = *56·5*
(f) 71·3 + 8·2 = *79·5*

Go to Textbook page 54.

15 Decimals: subtraction using a calculator

Race score cards

1 (a) Complete each score by subtracting course and time penalty points from race points.
(b) Add to find the total score for each boat.

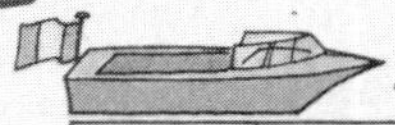

Sprite

	Race points	Course penalty	Time penalty	Score
1	38·5	0·7	0·4	37·4
2	55·3	1·5	0·5	53·3
3	38·4	4·8	1·9	31·7
			Total score	122·4

Dawn

	Race points	Course penalty	Time penalty	Score
1	42·6	1·6	0·8	40·2
2	58·0	0·9	0·3	56·8
3	34·2	3·0	1·2	30·0
			Total score	127·0

Imp

	Race points	Course penalty	Time penalty	Score
1	41·6	2·1	0·7	38·8
2	61·0	1·2	0·3	59·5
3	32·2	2·4	1·2	28·6
			Total score	126·9

Storm

	Race points	Course penalty	Time penalty	Score
1	41·7	0·7	0·3	40·7
2	50·1	1·5	0·3	48·3
3	39·1	4·8	2·6	31·7
			Total score	120·7

Hope

	Race points	Course penalty	Time penalty	Score
1	40·5	1·6	0·9	38·0
2	54·5	0·3	0·5	53·7
3	37·2	3·0	2·6	31·6
			Total score	123·3

Fairwind

	Race points	Course penalty	Time penalty	Score
1	35·7	2·1	0·2	33·4
2	52·6	1·2	0·5	50·9
3	42·6	2·4	1·9	38·3
			Total score	122·6

2 The winner is the boat with the highest total score. Which boat wins? *Dawn*

Go to Textbook page 57.

16 Length: measuring in centimetres, perimeter

Swimming awards badges

1 For each of these badges
- measure the lengths of the sides
- find the perimeter.

(a) 5 cm, 3 cm, 3 cm, 5 cm

Perimeter = 5 + 5 + 3 + 3
= 16 cm

(b) 4 cm, 4 cm, 6 cm

Perimeter = 4 + 4 + 6
= 14 cm

(c) 5 cm, 3 cm, 3 cm, 8 cm

Perimeter = 19 cm

(d) 4 cm, 4 cm, 4 cm

Perimeter = 12 cm

(e) 7cm, 3cm, 3cm, 7cm

Perimeter = 20 cm

(f) 2cm, 2cm, 2cm, 2cm, 2cm

Perimeter = 10 cm

Go to Textbook page 69.

17
Line symmetry

Krazy kites

1 Draw **all** the lines of symmetry each shape has.
The first one is done for you.

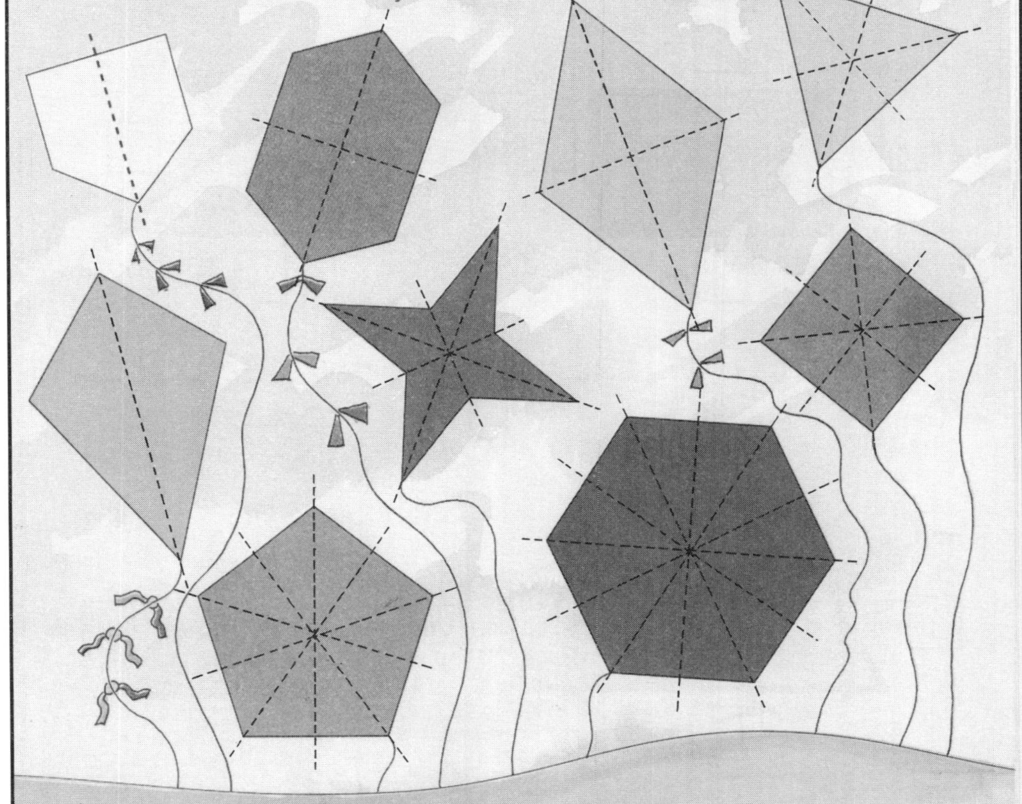

Problem solving

2 Colour so that each design has **only** the lines of symmetry shown.

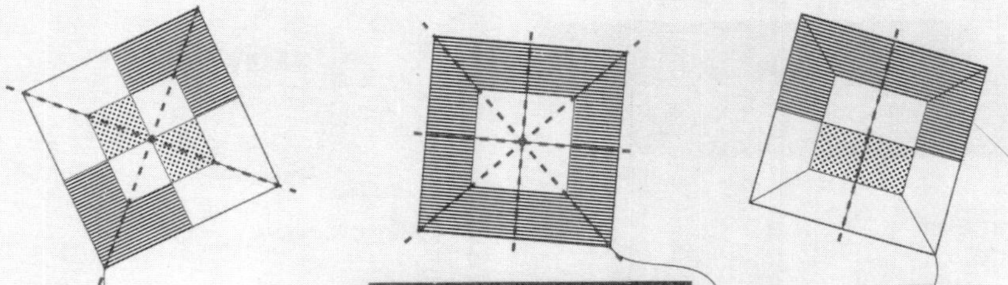

Go to Textbook page 97.

Other shadings are possible.

18
Line symmetry: cut outs

Shapes for use with Textbook page 96.

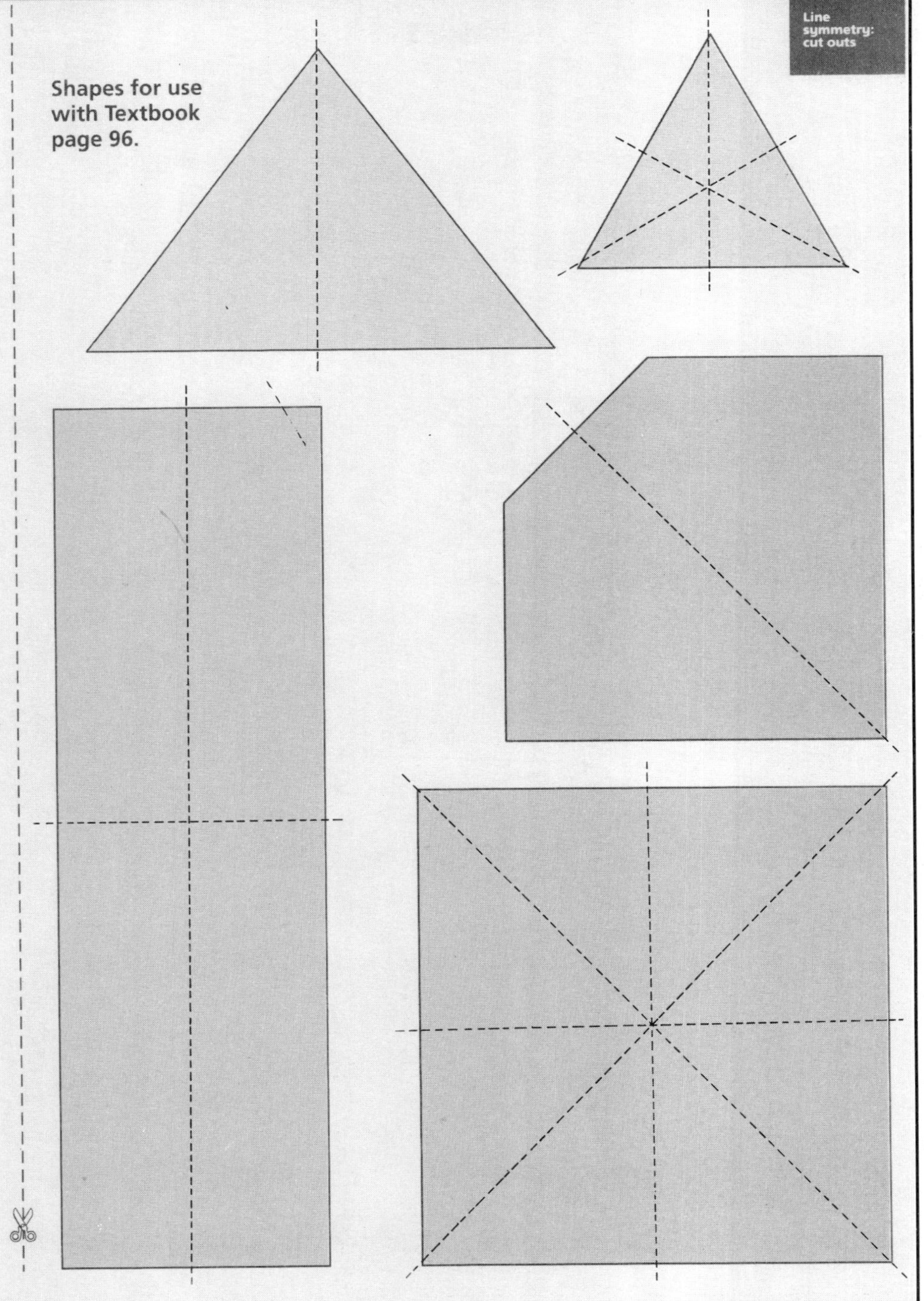

22 Angles: comparison

Clouds

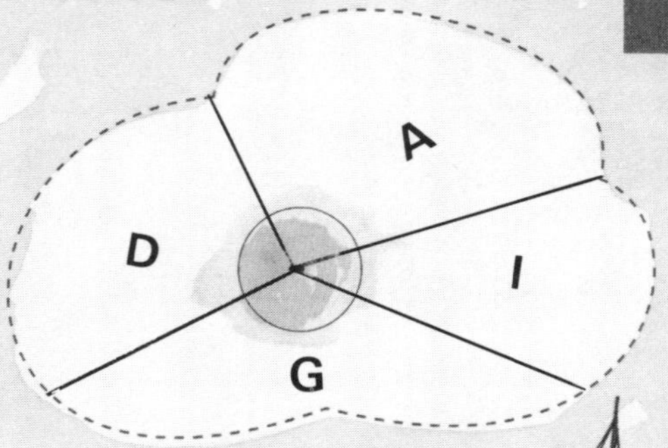

1 (a) Cut out all the angles from **Workbook page 20.**

(b) Compare pairs of angles by putting one on top of the other.
Arrange all the angles in order of size.

(c) List the angles, in order, starting with the smallest.

F, K, I, J, B, H, D, A, E, G, C

(d) Stick the four white angles around the point in the middle of the sun to make the cloud above.

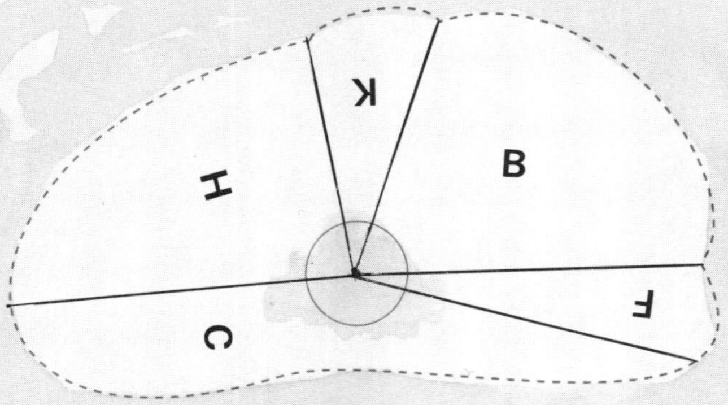

2 Stick the five grey angles around the moon to make this cloud.

3 Stick the two orange angles together to make this cloud.

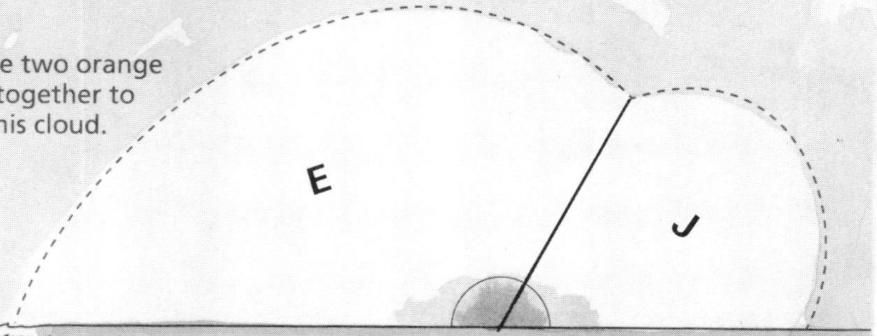

Go to Textbook page 103.

24 Tiling

Cathy's cards

Cathy designs greetings cards using shapes to make tilings.

Draw and colour shapes to complete the tiling on each card.

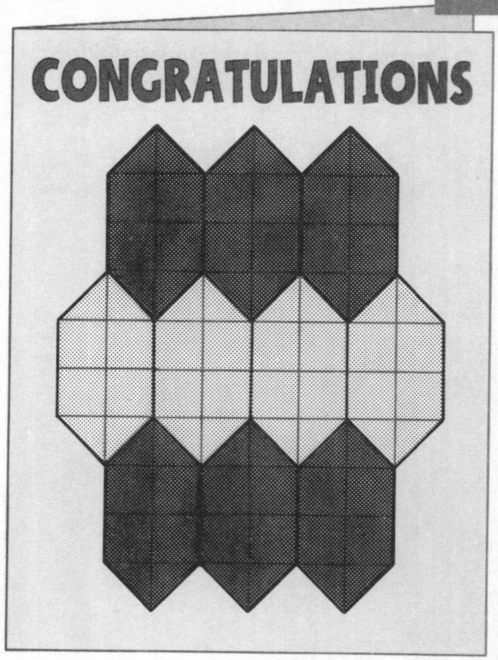

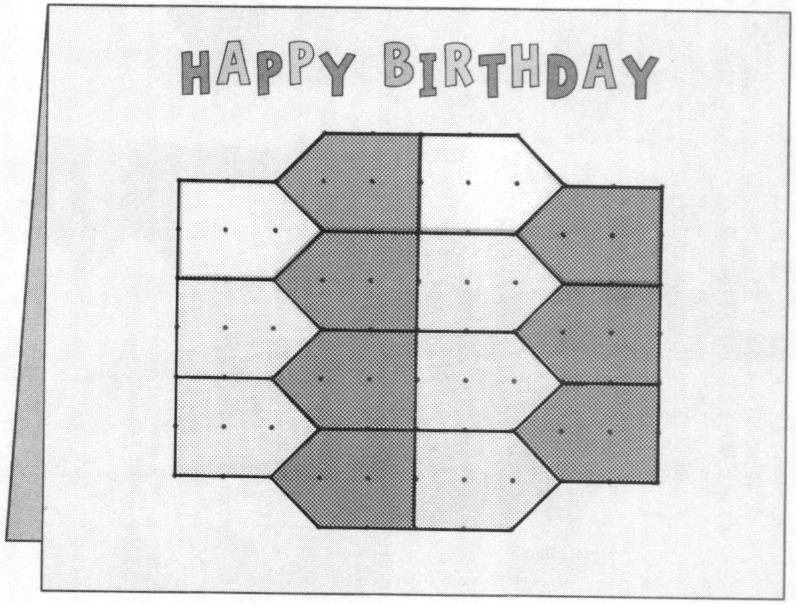

25
Tiling

Special occasions

Complete each card design by making a tiling. Use the given shape.

Hexagon

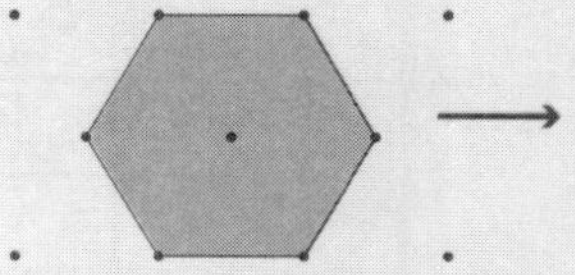

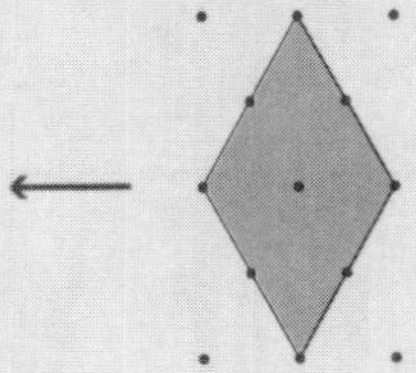

Rhombus

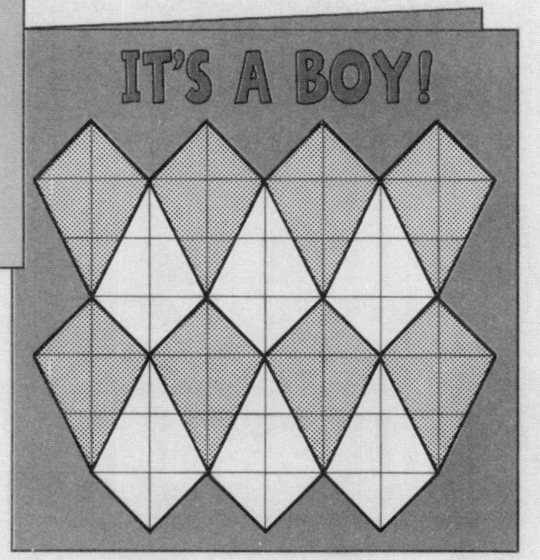

Kite

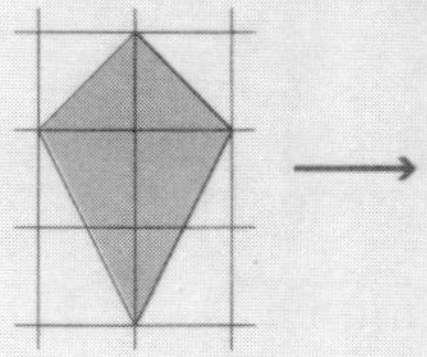

26
Tiling

Design a card

1 Help Cathy make a design for each card using the shape given.

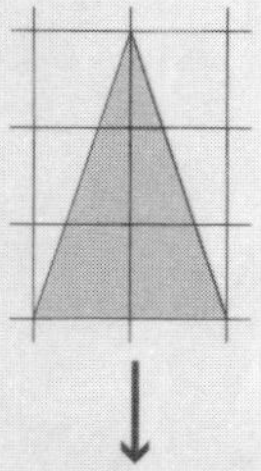

2 Design some cards of your own which have tiling patterns.

Ask your teacher what to do next.

27
Area: Irregular shapes

Nature trail

1 The Junior Rangers find these pieces of litter on the nature trail.
Find the approximate area of each.

(a)

Area: about *7* cm²

(b)

Area: *about 8cm²*

(c)

Area: *about 11cm²*

2 Find the approximate area of each of these.

(a) **Owl feather**

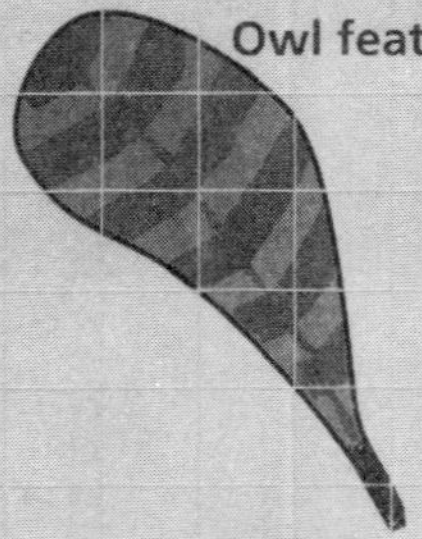

Area: *about 8cm²*

(b) **Duck feather**

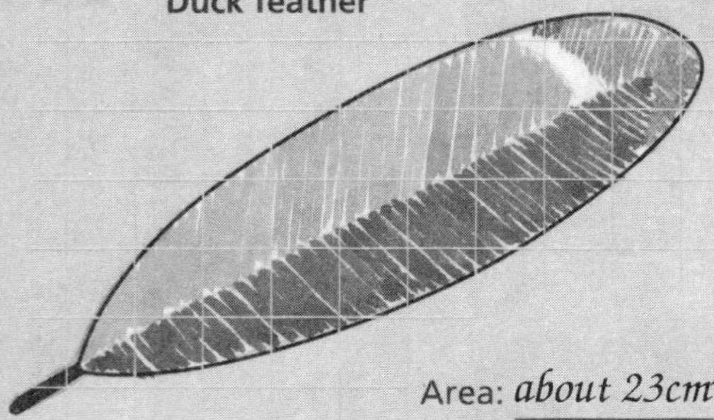

Area: *about 23cm²*

(c) **Beech leaf**

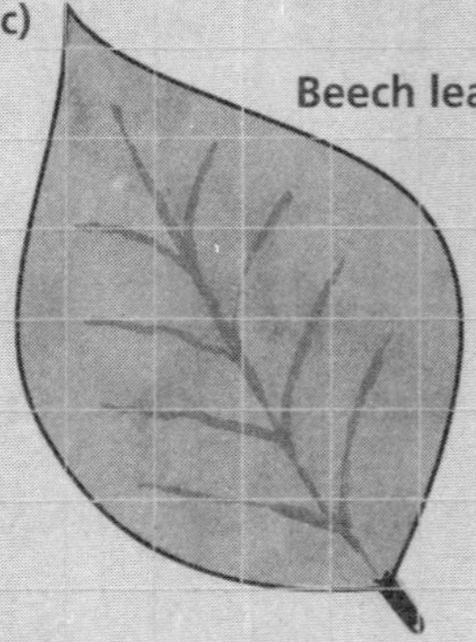

Area: *about 22cm²*

(d) **Oak leaf**

Area: *about 14cm²*

28
Area: Irregular shapes

On the right track

1 Dan spotted these footprints on the trail.
Find the approximate area of each.

(a) **Duck**

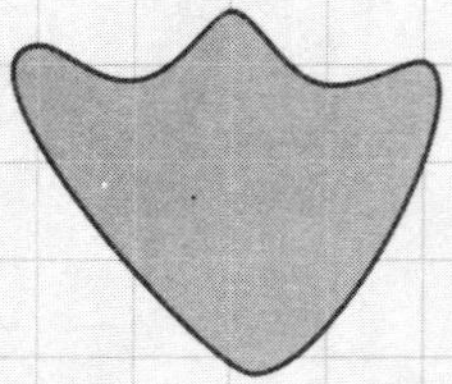

Area: *about 9cm²*

(b) **Wildcat**

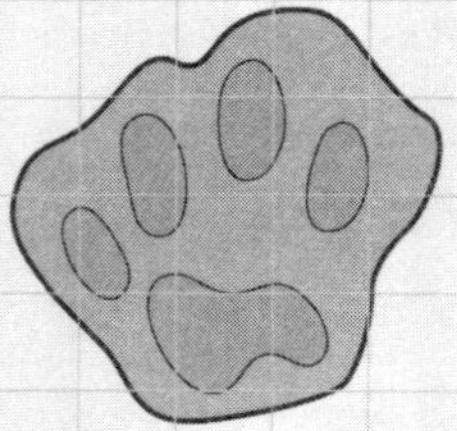

Area: *about13cm²*

2 Draw 2 animal or bird footprints. Write the area of each.

Answers depend on the children's drawings.

3 **(a)** Draw an animal or bird footprint with an area of about 20 cm².
(b) Ask a friend to check its area.

Answers depend on the children's drawings.

4 Draw your own footprint on centimetre squared paper.
Find the approximate area of your footprint.

Area: *Answers depend on the children.*

Ask your teacher what to do next.

29 Weight: scales

Growfast

Professor Kluless is making Growfast Fertilizer.

1 On the scales, draw pointers to show the weight of each ingredient.

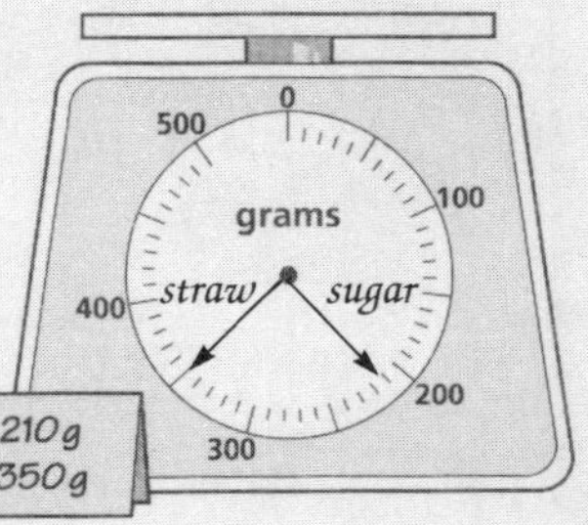

sugar 210g
straw 350g

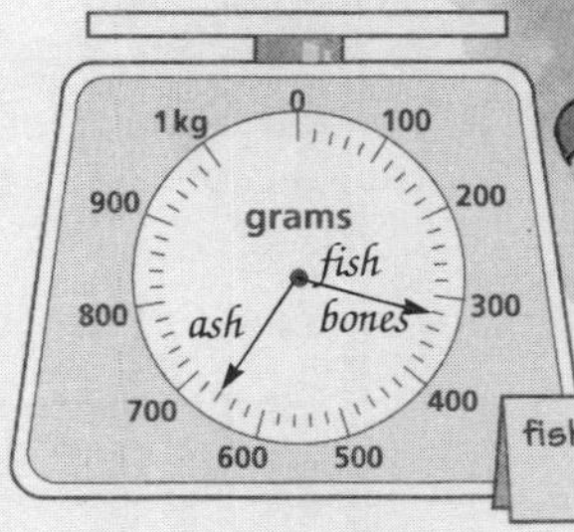

fish bones 320g
ash 660g

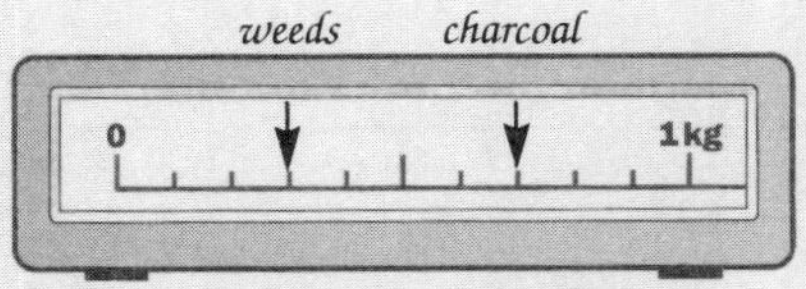

weeds 300g
charcoal 700g

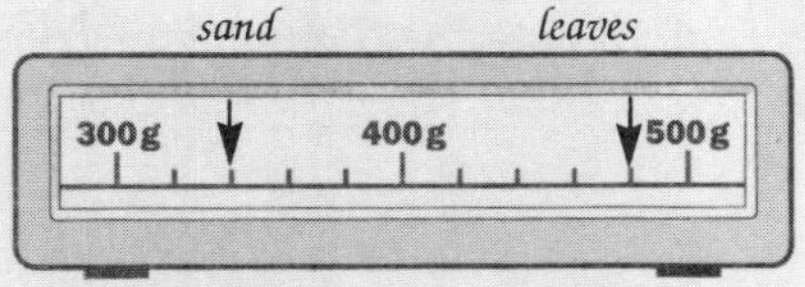

sand 340g
leaves 480g

2 He also uses these ingredients.

For each
- choose **one** of the scales
- draw a pointer to show its weight.

mushrooms 580g
bark 650g
chalk 370g

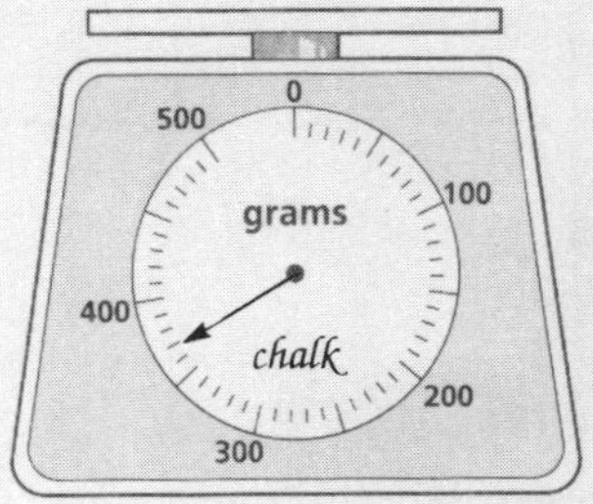

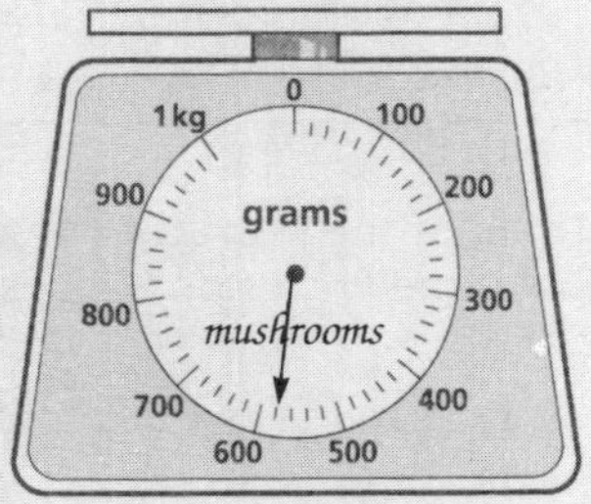

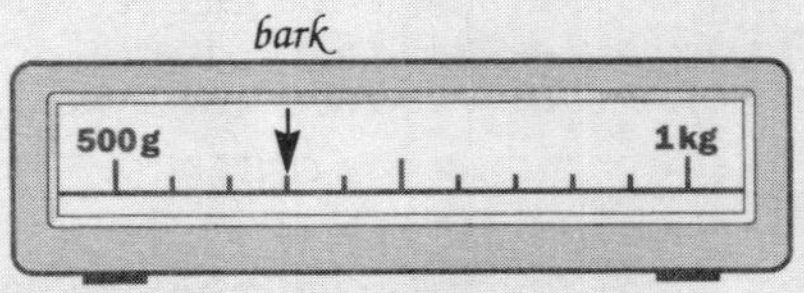

30 Weight: addition, subtraction

The Professor's shopping

The weedkiller and the bulb fibre have a total weight of 1550g
= 1000g + 550g
= **1kg 550g**

$$\begin{array}{r} 700g \\ +\ 850g \\ \hline 1550g \end{array}$$ or **1kg 550g**

1 Write the total weights, in kg and g, of

slug pellets and plant food *1kg 250g* $\begin{array}{r} 650g \\ +600g \\ \hline 1250g \end{array}$

ant powder and bulb fibre *1kg 100g* $\begin{array}{r} 250g \\ -\ 850g \\ \hline 1100g \end{array}$

grass seed and charcoal *2kg 300g* $\begin{array}{r} 1500g \\ +800g \\ \hline 2300g \end{array}$

sand and seed potatoes *3kg 500g* $\begin{array}{r} 1800g \\ +1700g \\ \hline 3500g \end{array}$

The difference in weight between the grass seed and the charcoal is 700g.

$$\begin{array}{r} 1500g \\ -\ 800g \\ \hline 700g \end{array}$$

2 Find the difference in weight between the

sand and weedkiller $\begin{array}{r} 1800g \\ -\ 700g \\ \hline 1100g \end{array}$ *= 1kg 100g*

seed potatoes and bulb fibre $\begin{array}{r} 1700g \\ -\ 850g \\ \hline 850g \end{array}$

Problem solving

3 The Professor carries all nine items in 3 shopping bags. Each bag cannot hold more than 3 kg.

Write what he can carry in each bag.

One possible solution is:

There are other correct solutions.

Go to Textbook page 79.

31 Measure: reading scales

Return from Planet Kylor

Professor Kluless and Zantha are getting ready to return to Earth with plants from Planet Kylor.

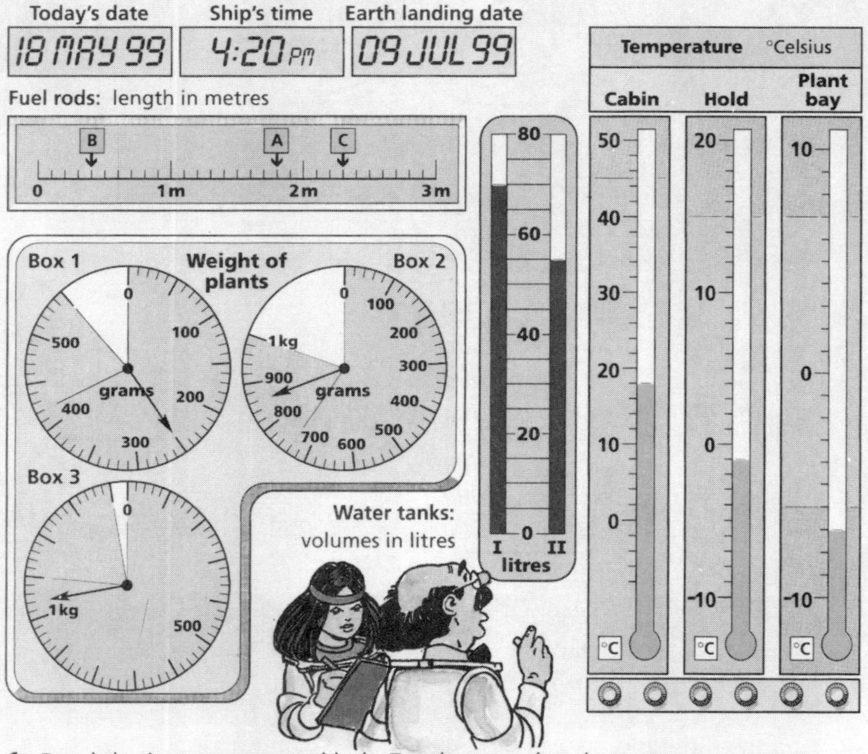

1 Read the instruments and help Zantha complete her report.

INSTRUMENT READINGS

(a) Today's date: *18* / *05* / *99* (b) Time: *4.20* pm

(c) Temperature: Cabin *18* °C Hold *⁻1°C* Plant bay *⁻7°C*

(d) Fuel rod length: A *1·8* m B *0·4m* C *2·3m*

(e) Weight of plants: Box 1 *250* g Box 2 *860g* Box 3 *1040g or 1kg 40g*

(f) Volume of water: Tank I *70* l Tank II *55l*

Zantha.

32 Measure: reading scales, problems

Danger zones

1 Use Zantha's report. Find

(a) the total length of the 3 fuel rods *4·5m*

(b) the difference in weight between the plants in Boxes 2 and 3 *180g*

(c) how much time they have left before Earth Control calls the ship at 5.35 pm *1hr 15mins*

2 (a) How many days are left before landing on Earth? *52 days (51, 53 acceptable)*

(b) Together they use 1 litre of water each day. How many litres will be left when they land? *73l (72, 74 acceptable depending on 2(a))*

3 The red parts of the instrument scales indicate danger. Complete the danger zones report.

DANGER ZONES

(a) Fuel rod lengths: *0·6 metres or shorter*

(b) Weight of plants: Box 1 *420g or heavier*

Box 2 *740g or heavier* Box 3 *1kg 100g or heavier*

(c) Cabin temperature *45°C or hotter*

Hold temperature *15°C or warmer*

Plant bay temperature *7°C or warmer*

⁻7°C or colder

4 Three of the instructions show readings in the danger zone. Warn the Professor. Suggest what he might do.

1. *Fuel rod B is too short. Fit a new fuel rod.*
2. *Plant Box 2 is too heavy. Take out at least 120g of plants and put them in Box 1.*
3. *Plant bay is too cold. Increase temperature to more than ⁻7°C.*

33
Measure: problems

Plants and seeds

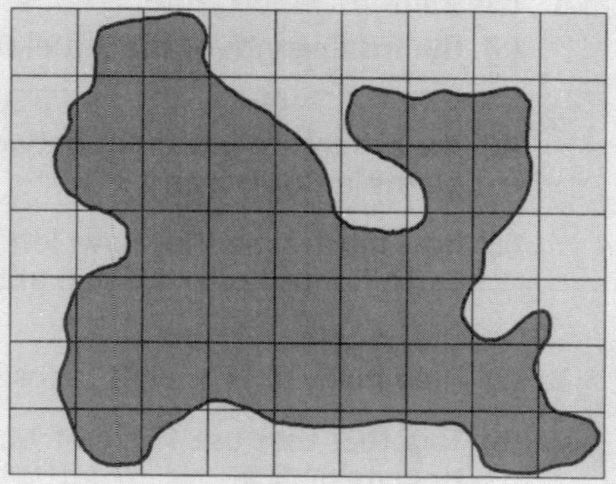

1 (a) Find the area in cm^2 of this green fungus from Planet Kylor.

about 35cm²

(b) The fungus weighs 1 g. It **doubles** its weight every day. After how many days will it weigh more than 2 kg?

11 days

2 The drawing shows 1 cm^3 plastic boxes used for storing seeds from Planet Kylor.

Find the total volume of the boxes.

32cm³

3 This instrument warns of approaching meteors.
(a) Label the rest of the scale.
(b) Colour a red danger zone for distances of 40 metres or less.

Meteor warning

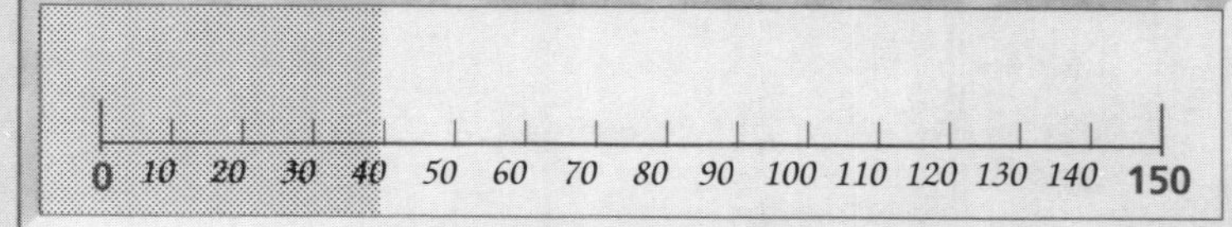

Distance in metres

Ask your teacher what to do next.

34
Handling data: grouped tallies

Tree survey

The red group made a survey of 100 trees in Atholl Wood. They identified the trees by their leaves.

These are red group's survey notes.

Red group *Pam and Wes*

O O B S B B O A O S B
S A S B O S A O B S A
A B A B B B B B O S B
A O O B A O B A O A O
S S B B O O A S A S

Red group *Li and Jan*

B A B S B A A A B A O
O A B S A O S B S A A
B A O A O B S B A A B
S S B O A O S A B B O
B B

1 Use tally marks grouped in fives (卌) to complete this table.

	Tally marks	Number of trees
oak	卌 卌 卌 卌 II	22
sycamore	卌 卌 卌 IIII	19
beech	卌 卌 卌 卌 卌 卌 II	32
ash	卌 卌 卌 卌 卌 II	27

2 Complete the graph.

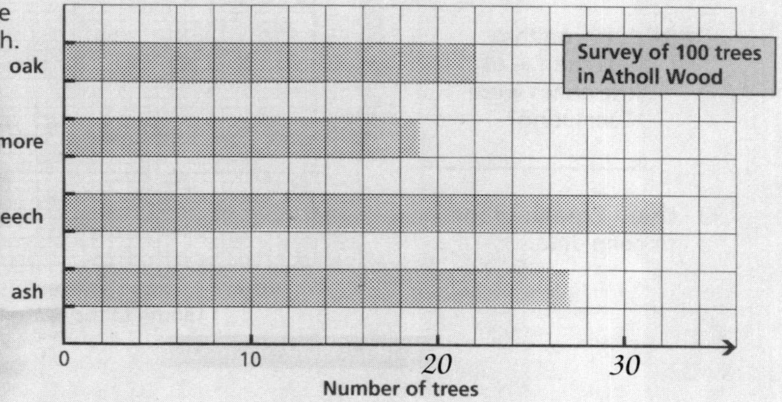

35
Handling data: grouped tallies

Cones

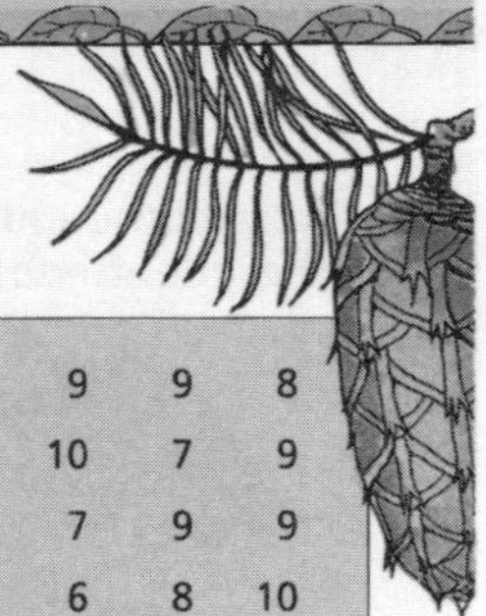

The blue group measured the lengths of 120 fir cones.

Lengths of cones to the nearest centimetre

														9	9	8
6	9	9	8	7	8	7	9	8	7	9	8	8	6	10	7	9
6	8	7	9	6	8	9	10	8	7	9	6	8	8	7	9	9
10	7	8	7	9	8	6	8	7	8	8	10	7	9	6	8	10
8	7	8	7	9	9	8	10	6	8	9	7	9	8	7	10	9
6	8	9	10	8	6	7	9	9	7	6	8	6	8	8	7	8
6	8	7	8	6	9	7	8	8	10	7	8	8	6	8	8	7
8	9	10	7	6	8	9	8	9	10	7	9	7	9	6		

1 Complete the table using blue group's information.

Length of cone	Tally marks	Number of cones
6 cm	卌 卌 卌 II	*17*
7 cm	卌 卌 卌 卌 卌	*25*
8 cm	卌 卌 卌 卌 卌 卌 卌 IIII	*39*
9 cm	卌 卌 卌 卌 卌 III	*28*
10 cm	卌 卌 I	*11*

2 **(a)** Which was the most common length of cone found?

8cm

(b) Is it true that less than $\frac{1}{10}$ of the cones were 10 cm long?

yes

3 Draw a graph of the fir cone data.

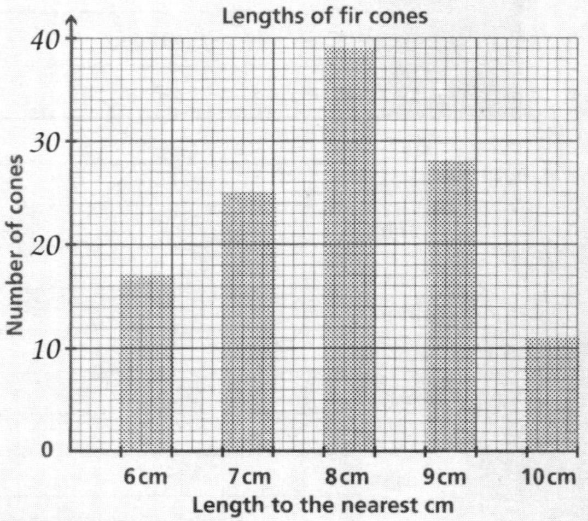

Go to Textbook page 116.

36
Handling data: surveys

Collecting clues

Ask your teacher which two areas to survey.
Use this sheet to record your findings.
Make a zig-zag book to compare the two survey areas.

Date	Time	Weather

Answers depend on the timing of the practical work.

	Area 1	Area 2
plants 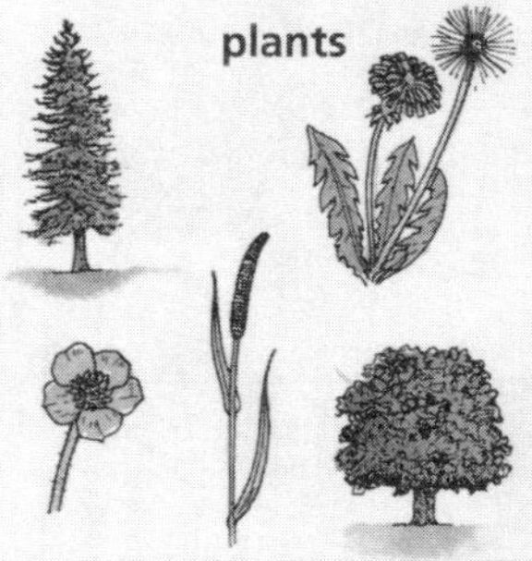		*Answers depend on the areas chosen for the survey.*
animals 		
pollution 		

Go to Textbook page 117.

E1 Making cubes

Practical work

E2 Four-digit numbers

1 (a) 3785
(b) 4684
(c) 1935

2 *Kittiwake* costs £3968
Eider costs £4249
Tern costs £1874
Fulmar costs £4575

E3 Four-digit numbers – continued

1 (a) No answer

(b)

Enter	2 4 5 1	to give	2451.
Press	+ 4 =	to give	2455.
Press	− 2 0 =	to give	2435.
Press	+ 7 0 0 =	to give	3135.
Press	+ 4 0 0 0 =	to give	7135.
Enter	8 9 3 6	to give	8936.
Press	+ 1 =	to give	8937.
Press	+ 1 0 =	to give	8947.
Press	− 9 0 0 =	to give	8047.
Press	− 5 0 0 0 =	to give	3047.

Four-digit numbers – continued E3

(c) 6185.
− 4 =
+ 20 =
+ 200 =
+ 3000 = 9401.

2 (a) The answer is always 3087.
(b) The answer is always 6174.
(c) The answer for 3-digit numbers with consecutive digits is always 198.
Three-digit numbers with consecutive **odd** or **even** digits always give the answer 396.

Training E4

1 (a) purple, pink, orange
(b) brown, yellow, purple
(c) purple

2 (a) Monday, Tuesday, Thursday evenings
(b) Wednesday, Thursday, Saturday evenings
(c) Thursday evening

3 I was left out of skills training.
2 were left out of 5-a-side.
7 were left out of circuit training.

4 (a) Tuesday and Friday
(b) 5 children who want to attend on Monday could be moved, as follows:
1 to Wednesday, 2 to Thursday and 2 to Saturday.
(This gives the following totals:

Mon	Tue	Wed	Thu	Fri	Sat
230	250	200	230	290	180)

There are other correct answers.

E5 Play ball

1 297, 78, 57, 498, 33, 81, 789

2

Numbers which divide exactly by 3	Sum of digits	Numbers which do not divide exactly by 3	Sum of digits
297	18	104	5
78	15	95	14
57	12	82	10
498	21	695	20
33	6	53	8
81	9		
789	24		

3 (a) They all divide exactly by 3.
(b) If the sum of the digits divides exactly by 3, then the number will also divide exactly by 3.

4 777, 102 and 819 will divide exactly by 3.

5 (a) 75, 801 and 132 will divide exactly by 3.
(b) Answers depend on the numbers chosen by the children.

E6 Stars

1 (a) Any 3-digit number made up from the given digits but with 5 as its unit digit.
(b) Any number from this set:
124, 312, 324, 412, 512, 524
(c) Any 3-digit number, made up from the given digits, whose sum of digits divides exactly by 3.
Possible answers include 123, 453, 531…

Stars – *continued* E6

2 (a) Divide the outer number by the inner one.
(b)

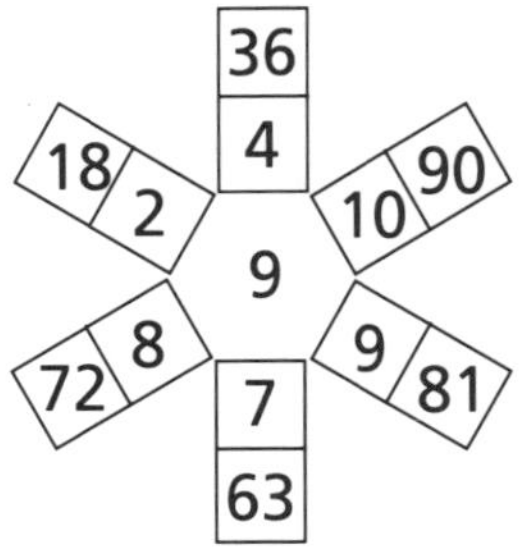

3 (a)

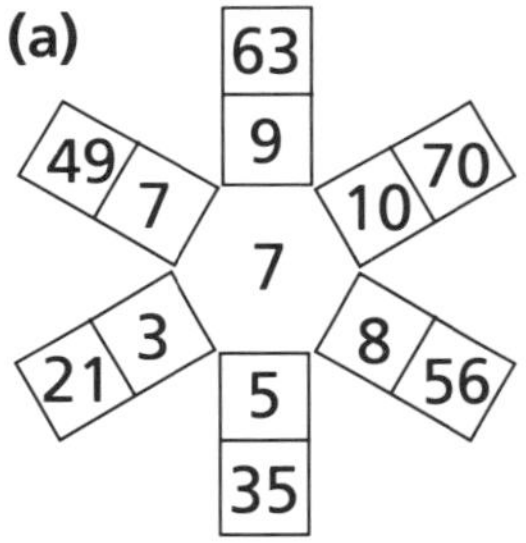

(b)

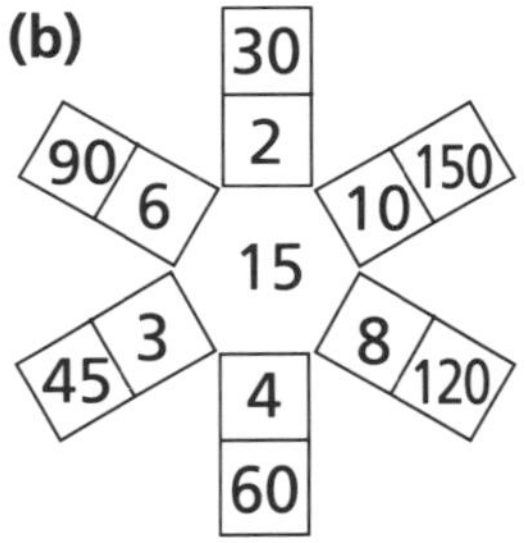

(c)

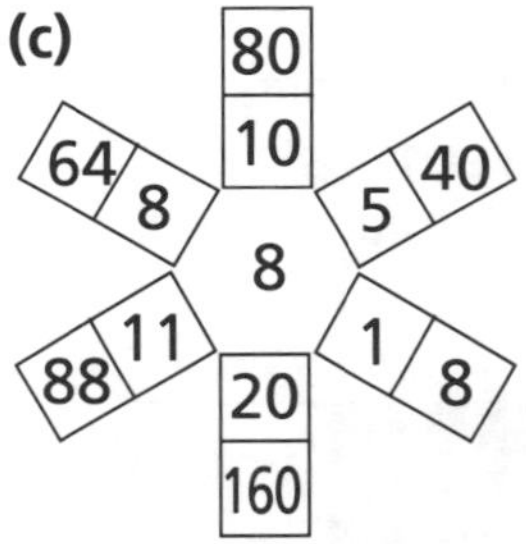

4 (a) Shelley Diamond is 36 years old.
(b) Burt Westwood is 56 years old.

The shape of it E7

1 Y, Z, 2, 3, 6, 7

2 HOW MANY SIDES HAS A PENTAGON?
It has 5 sides.

3 (a)  (60) or  (sixty)

(b)  (cuboid)

4 (a) SQUARE (b) CUBE
(c) CYLINDER (d) KITE
(e) SPHERE (f) CONE

E8 Kluless puzzles

1 (a) 715 (b) 723
(c) 127 (d) 7068

2 Various answers are possible. Some possibilities are:
(a) Add 500 to 625 (b) Subtract 100 from 1225 (c) Multiply 225 by 5

3 (a) 1379
(b) 285
(c) 75
(d) 9
(e) 536
(f) 662
(g) 6

E9 Mind stretchers

1

39		54		10		40		22
	Beat the clock							
10		9		27		19		10

2

[1] 3	6		[2] 5	8	
5		[3] 6	6		
0			[4] 1	[5] 7	
	[6] 4	1		[7] 5	[8] 7
[9] 1	0		[10] 1		8
	5		5		

3

[1] 4	2		[2] 3	7	[3] 7
0		[4] 5	0		8
0		[5] 4	0	1	
	[6] 1				[7] 8
[8] 2	0			[9] 2	8
	5		[10] 4	4	

E10 The school café

1

raisins, apple	15p
raisins, yogurt	21p
raisins, nuts	26p
apple, yogurt	24p
apple, nuts	29p

2

raisins, apple, yogurt	30p
raisins, apple, nuts	35p
raisins, apple, roll	45p
raisins, apple, orange juice	50p
raisins, yogurt, nuts	41p
raisins, yogurt, roll	51p
apple, yogurt, nuts	44p
apple, yogurt, roll	54p

3

raisins, raisins, roll	42p
raisins, raisins, juice	47p
raisins, raisins, yogurt	27p
raisins, raisins, apple	21p
raisins, raisins, nuts	32p
nuts, nuts, raisins,	46p
nuts, nuts, apple	49p
apple, apple, yogurt	33p
apple, apple, raisins	24p
apple, apple, nuts	38p
apple, apple, roll	48p
yogurt, yogurt, nuts	50p
yogurt, yogurt, apple	39p
yogurt, yogurt, raisins	36p

E11 Magic squares

1 Yes, they are magic.
The numbers in each row, column and diagonal of Square P add up to 130·5.
The numbers in each row, column and diagonal of Square Q add up to 113·4.

2 (a) Each pair has a difference of 5·7
(b) Each pair has a difference of 5·7

3 (a) Each pair has a difference of 5·7
(b) Answer depends on the child. The actual difference will again be 5·7
(c) Add 5·7 to each number in Square Q.

4 (a)

7·8	1·3	10·4
9·1	6·5	3·9
2·6	11·7	5·2

(b)

54·6	9·1	72·8
63·7	45·5	27·3
18·2	81·9	36·4

(c) Yes, it is magic.
The sum of each row, column and diagonal is 136·5

E12 Wonderpark

1 (a) 378 (b) 504 (c) 735 (d) 882

2 (a) 286 (b) 651 (c) 588 (d) 630

3 1 x 27 = 27
2 x 27 = 54
4 x 27 = 108
8 x 27 = 216
16 x 27 = 432
32 x 27 = 864
(a) 918 (b) 351 (c) 513 (d) 675
(e) 621 (f) 783 (g) 810 (h) 729

Wonderpark – *continued* E13

1 (a) 450 (b) 525

2 (a) 420 (b) 408 (c) 688 (d) 837

3 (a) 858 (b) 418

4 (a) 928 (b) 897 (c) 882 (d) 944

Squares and rectangles E14

1 (a) The area of each shape is 9 cm^2.
(b) This is one correct solution:

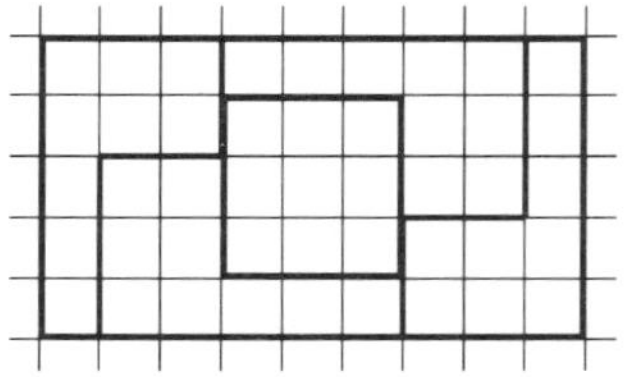

(c) The area of the rectangle is 45 cm^2.

2 (a) Practical work

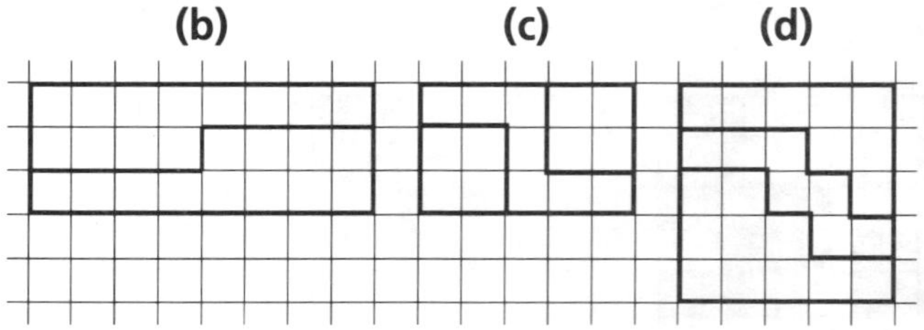

Area = 25 cm^2

E15 Squares and rectangles – *continued*

1 (a) Practical work

(b)

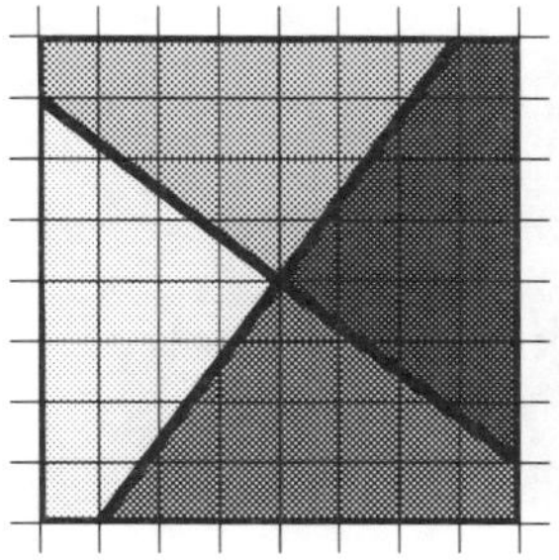

(c) 64 cm^2

(d) 16 cm^2

2 (a) Practical work

(b) Two possible arrangements are:

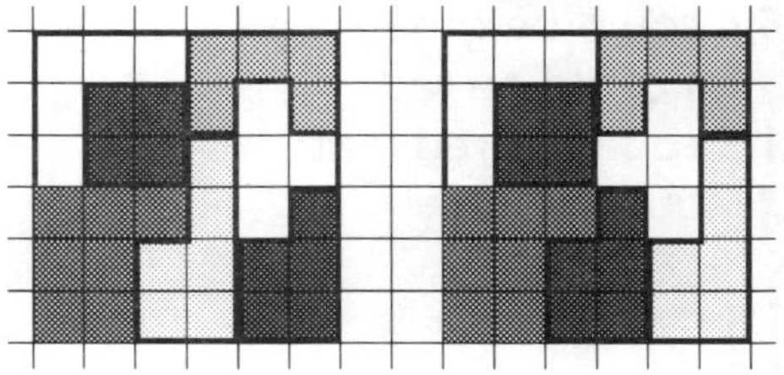

(c) Two possible arrangements are:

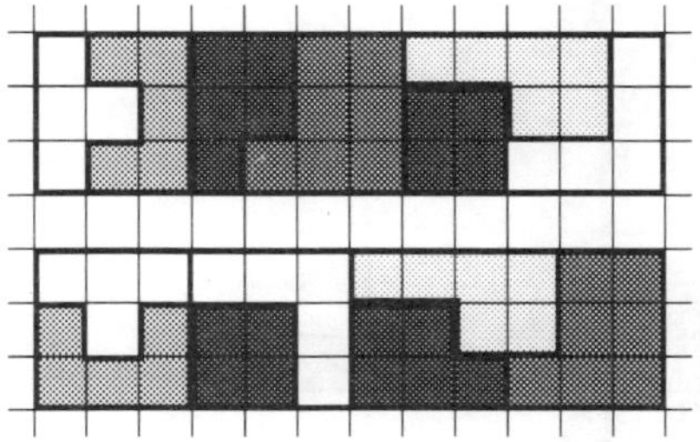

(d) The area of both the square and the rectangle is 36 cm^2.
The perimeter of the square is 24 cm and the perimeter of the rectangle is 30 cm.

Inspector Horse investigates E16 & E17

1 *Miss Marble*
Arrived in Cardale at *10.25am*.
Met Mr Holmes at about *12.25pm*.
Arrived back in Aimsley at *2.40pm*.

Ms Blake
Took the *1.30pm* bus to Bryton arriving at *1.55pm*.
Left the dentist at about *2.25pm*.

Mr Holmes
Met Miss Marble at about *12.25pm* in Cardale.
Returned to Aimsley at *2.40pm*.

Mr Baggart
Took the *11.30am* bus from Aimsley to Cardale.
Left Cardale at *12.45pm*.
Arrived in Aimsley at *1.40pm*.

2 Mr Baggart had the opportunity to commit the crime.
He was the only one in Aimsley between *1.30pm* and *2.38pm*.

The Plaza Theatre E18

1 £20·46

2 £20·46

3 (a) £23·39
(b) £26·23
(c) £58·05

4 (a) £18·45
(b) £27·60

5 £22·56

E19 Boxes challenge

1 **(a)** $10cm^3$ **(b)** $100cm^3$

2 **(a)**, **(b)**, **(c)** } Answers depend on the objects chosen by the children.

3 **(a)**, **(b)** } Answers depend on the boxes available.

4 Two possible answers using 8 'longs' are:

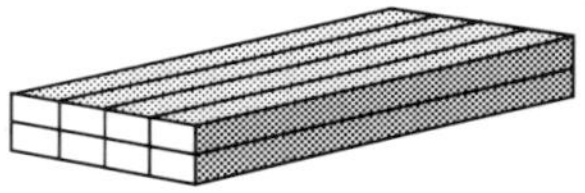

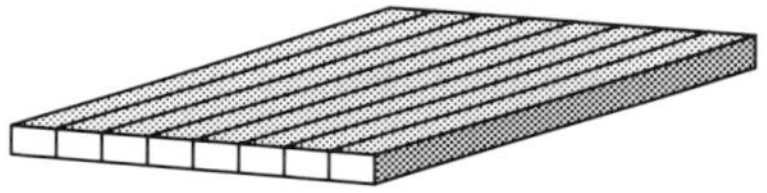

There are other correct solutions using 1 cm^3 cubes.

5 A possible answer using 12 'longs' is:

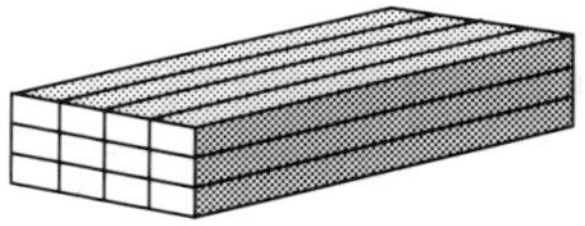

There are other correct solutions using 1 cm^3 cubes.

Alex's window designs E20

1 **(a), (b)**

8		G		R		B
7	G		R		B	
6		R		B		
5	R		G			G
4	R		G			G
3		R		B		
2	G		R		B	
1		G		R		B
	1	2	3	4	5	6

This is the line of symmetry (dashed line between rows 5 and 4)

2 **(a)** 2,4 could be blue *or* 2,3 could be red *and* 5,2 could be green *or* 5,5 could be blue.
(b) 3,1 could be blue *or* 6,4 could be green *and* 3,3 could be green *or* 4,4 could be red.
(c) 3,1 could be blue *or* 1,3 could be red *and* 5,2 could be red *or* 2,5 could be blue.

3 **(a)** red: 5,7 5,8 6,7 6,8
blue: 3,3 3,4 4,5 4,6
green: 1,1 1,2 2,1 2,2

(b) red: 1,1 4,5
blue: 2,2 2,3 5,6 5,7
green: 3,4 6,8

(c) red: 1,1 1,2 6,1 6,2 6,7 6,8
blue: 2,2 2,3 5,2 5,3 5,6 5,7
green: 3,3 3,4 4,3 4,4 4,5 4,6

E21 Folding rectangles

1 **(a) (b) (c)** Practical work
(d) The shape is a rhombus.

2 Practical work
(a) a hexagon
(b) square of side 6 cm
(c) 'flower' shape or 'cloud' shape

3 Practical work

4 Practical work

E22 Red tape

1 **(a)** Practical drawing work

(b) Practical work

(c) Answer depends on the children's selection of objects.

2 18 cm 22 cm 20 cm

3 28 cm

The 'Stepping Stones' E23

1 Gem is 7 years old.
Ruby is 8 years old.
Rocky is 9 years old.
Flint is 10 years old.

2 Gem weighs 30 kilograms.
Flint and Rocky each weigh 40 kilograms.
Ruby weighs 50 kilograms.

3 Gem lives in cave number 38.
Ruby lives in cave number 40.
Flint lives in cave number 42.
Rocky lives in cave number 44.

What's your angle? E24

1 **(a), (b)** Practical work

2 Angle

A	between 45° and 90°
B	about 90°
C	less than 45°
D	about 90°
E	about 45°
F	about 45°
G	between 45° and 90°
H	more than 90°
I	about 90°
J	about 90°

3 (Game)

E25 Another angle

1

Angle	Estimate	Check
B	between 45° and 90°	✓
C	about 90°	✓
D	more than 90°	✓
E	less than 45°	✓

2 **(a), (b)** Practical work

3 **(a), (b)** Practical work

(c)

Angle	Estimate	Check
F	less than 45°	✓
G	more than 90°	✓
H	about 45°	✓

(d) Answers depend on triangles drawn by the children.

E26 Egyptian hieroglyphics

1 **(a)** 14 **(b)** 33 **(c)** 210 **(d)** 111 **(e)** 2638 **(f)** 5205

2 **(a)**  **(b)**  **(c)** 

(d) 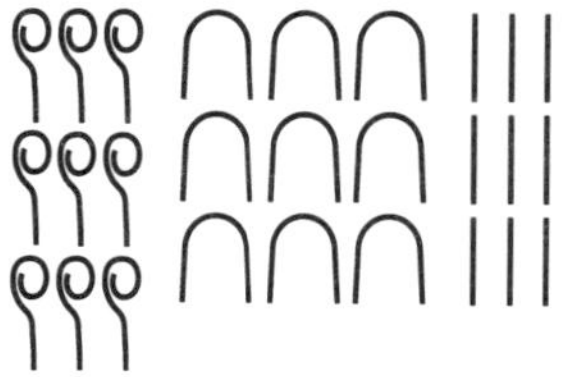 **(e)** 

3 **(a)** Answer depends on the children's ages.

(b) 

(c)
(d) } Answers depend on the child.
(e)

Egyptian hieroglyphics – *continued* E26

4 **(a)** 

(b) 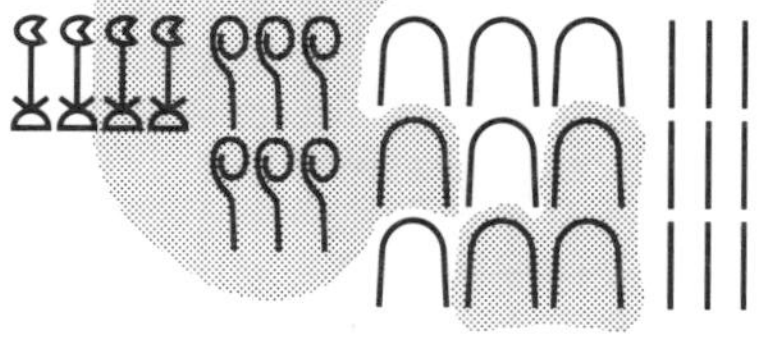

5 **(a)**  (48 + 626 = 674)

(b) 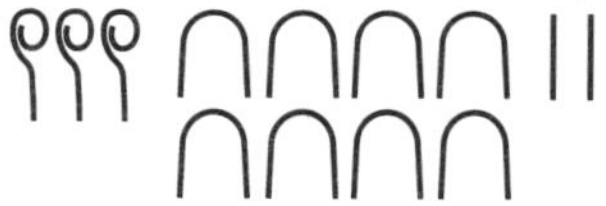 (1000 – 618 = 382)

Roman numerals E27

1 **(a)** 7 **(b)** 11 **(c)** 24

2 **(a)** Answers depend on the child's age.
(b) XII
(c) Answer depends on size of class.

3 **(a)** 52 **(b)** 70 **(c)** 111 **(d)** 560 **(e)** 2000

4 **(a)** LX **(b)** CLII **(c)** DLXX **(d)** MDCCC **(e)** MMDCXXXI

5 **(a)** 755 **(b)** 1666

E28 & E29 Bird cards

1 **(a)** chaffinch, sparrow
(b) barn owl, starling, sparrow, blackbird, swallow, robin
(c) chaffinch, sparrow, swallow, robin
(d) sparrow, swallow, robin

2 insects

3 **(a)** robin **(b)** blackbird

4 Answers depend on how children perceive colours of birds.

5 Practical work

6 Practical work

E30 Bird table

Practical work
Answers depend on the children's work.